The
Spirit of
Spring

The Spirit of Spring

A Tale of the Greek God Dionysos

BY PENELOPE PRODDOW

ILLUSTRATED BY SUSAN JEFFERS

Bradbury Press, Englewood Cliffs, New Jersey

For my mother and father

Copyright © 1970 by Penelope Proddow
Copyright © 1970 by Susan Jeffers
All rights reserved. No part of this book may be
reproduced in any form or by any means, except
for the inclusion of brief quotations in a review,
without permission in writing from the publisher.
Library of Congress Catalog Number: 76-104339
Manufactured in the United States of America
First printing   0-13-835397-2
Design by Susan Jeffers
The text of this book is set in 11pt. Elegante.
The illustrations are black and white wash paintings,
reproduced in halftone.

j P942 sp

CONTENTS

Characters

ALCITHOE	An old hag of Orchomenus
APHRODITE	The goddess of love
APOLLO	The god of music and archery
ARES	The god of war
ARIADNE	A Cretan princess, the wife of Dionysos
ARSIPPE	An old hag of Orchomenus
ARTEMIS	The goddess of the forest and the hunt
ATHAMAS	The husband of Ino
ATHENA	The goddess of wisdom
ATLAS	The father of the Hyades, a giant who held the heavens on his shoulders
BEROE	A servant of King Cadmus, actually Hera in disguise
BRIGHT EYES	A maenad
KING CADMUS	Semele's father, the king of Thebes
CERBERUS	The watchdog of Hades
CHARON	The old ferryman who takes the dead across the river Styx to Hades
DROPE	The mother of Pan
DRYADS	Tree nymphs

DIONYSOS	The god of vines and ivy and flowers and numerous woodland animals
DEMETER	The goddess of grain
HADES	The king of the land of the dead which takes its name from him
HARMONIA	Semele's mother, the queen of Thebes
HEPHESTOS	The god of the forge
HERA	The queen of the gods
HERMES	Zeus's messenger who was also the god of travelers
HYADES	The nurses of Dionysos
INO	A sister of Semele, who later becomes the white goddess of the sea, Leucothea
IRIS	Hera's messenger, the goddess of the rainbow
LEARCHOS	A son of Ino
LEUCONOE	An old hag of Orchomenus
MAENADS	The female followers of Dionysos
MELIKERTES	A son of Ino who later becomes the god of mariners, Palaimon
MIDAS	The king of Phrygia
MINYAS	The father of Leuconoe, Alcithoe and Arsippe
NAIADS	Water nymphs
NEREIDS	Sea nymphs
OREADS	Mountain nymphs

PAN	The god of the flocks and shepherds of Arcadia
PENTHEUS	The king of Thebes
PERSEPHONE	The queen of the dead
PHARAOH	The ruler of Egypt
POSEIDON	The god of the sea
POTAMIADS	River nymphs
RHEA	The goddess of the earth
SATYRS	Youthful creatures with the legs, tails, hooves and horns of a goat and the faces and torsos of men
SEASONS	The maidens Spring, Summer and Winter, guardians of the gates of Mount Olympus
SEMELE	Dionysos' mother, a Theban princess
SILENI	Corpulent, elderly creatures with the legs, tails, hooves and horns of a goat and the faces and torsos of men
SILENOS	Dionysos' tutor, the oldest of the sileni
STRIFE	The spirit of discord
TEIRESIAS	An old Theban seer
THESEUS	An Athenian hero who sailed to Crete to free his city from its yearly tribute
THETIS	A nymph of the sea
THYRBAS	A satyr
ZEUS	The king of the gods

A Godling Comes to Earth

CHAPTER ONE

"If your love is divine," said the old servant,
"ask him to appear to you in all his splendors."

*M*IGHTY ZEUS, KING OVER GODS AND MEN, SAT A long time ago in the throne room of his golden palace on Mount Olympus and watched the world revolve below. He was bored. He flicked his eyes over the Ethiopian plain, then along the western strand and back again to the Nile. He watched the circular patterns of earth—seasons swirling, animals wandering, plants blooming and withering. In contrast, life on the mountain peak seemed dull.

He was pondering this when his gaze, sweeping idly across the Greek mainland, paused at Thebes. Suddenly his whole face lit up. For there he beheld a golden-haired princess, at first so small that she had almost slipped from view. A regal himation embroidered with blue rosettes and many-colored peacocks covered her so completely that she would have looked like a bundle of priceless fabric had not her face, her hands and her little pale feet protruded. She was curled up alone in the women's chambers on a window bench, combing her hair and gazing up at the first evening stars. It was becoming so dark that Zeus could only see the

The Spirit of Spring

nails of her fingers glimmering as they moved the comb through her hair and gleaming like the shells on the Ionian Coast.

Night had been hovering gently over the earth, and now, like a giant bird, it sank down to rest, folding its black wings around Thebes and the palace as if to hide them from the probing eyes above. Such measures were to no avail, however, for Zeus's heart had already gone out to the Theban princess, and it was only a matter of time and planning before his royal person followed.

As soon as night descended, he jumped down from his throne onto his splendid mosaic floor. Crossing the chamber as quickly as his full robes would allow, he called out into the blackness for his messenger, Hermes.

His voice rang across the silence of the universe, and from the other side of the world Hermes heard the summons. Back over the Milky Way the messenger sped, his winged boots threading the stars of the air like the stepping stones of a rushing brook. He flew so high that even Olympus was far, far below, and would have faded into the darkness had not pinpricks of light shone from the torches lighting its gold-paved road. These he spied and began to circle down, weaving in and out among the nightclouds.

Touching Mount Olympus, Hermes skimmed over the royal road, first past the palaces of the lesser deities and then past the palaces of the major deities. As he rushed by, he saw gods feasting on ambrosia and drinking nectar. But it was not the time to linger,

A Godling Comes to Earth

for he had heard the urgency in his master's voice. With a final sprint, he covered the many steps of the palace of Zeus and streaked toward the throne room. He hurtled down the hall and just missed bumping into Zeus, who stood motionless at the threshold of the throne room, his face like a thundering sky, his eyes like snapping fire.

"Where on earth have you been?" the king of the gods exploded.

"In flight," gasped Hermes. "I haven't stopped for a single goblet of nectar."

"Then you're slowing down—I've walked all the way around the throne room waiting for you!"

Zeus motioned the bewildered herald to follow him inside.

"My lord," Hermes gathered his breath with difficulty. "I've never seen you looking so . . . so . . . distraught. . . ."

"Hermes!" Zeus interrupted him, for gods—even the king over gods—like mortals, become highly agitated when told they look the way they feel. Then he lowered his voice abruptly upon remembering the princess. "Hermes, we're losing time. . . ."

He leaned over his messenger and spoke. He whispered, for fear the echoing hall would toss the news into the winding corridors of the palace. What happened to plans once they trickled down the dim passageways, no one ever knew until the simplest of arrangements began to go awry.

"Tomorrow I wish to travel to Thebes."

"Thebes!" exclaimed the messenger.

"Shhh. . . ."

The Spirit of Spring

"Why Thebes?" whispered Hermes.

"I have just seen their princess."

"Ah," murmured Hermes. He understood now why Zeus was pacing back and forth and could not sit still a minute on his gold and ivory throne. Until Zeus reached Thebes and saw the princess again, every second would be a minute, every minute an hour, every hour a day and every day a week. On this new time scale, even his own swiftness would be as slow and tedious as an aged man poking along with a stick.

"Will she be as lovely on earth as she is when I gaze upon her from heaven?" Zeus asked eagerly. "Tell me, Hermes, for you have been a guest in the palace of her father, King Cadmus."

"She is as lovely as only a granddaughter of the goddess of love can be," Hermes answered.

"What is the princess' name?"

"Semele."

"Semele?"

"The wise men named her that from *Zembla,* which means *new earth,* for flowers burst into bloom when she was born."

"And her age?"

"She is very young, Zeus, and as prized in Thebes as myrtle and honey are in Athens."

"You have spoken well, Hermes. Now disguise me as a mortal, for I am going to Thebes at dawn."

As the hours passed, Hermes carefully removed the terrific powers, which Zeus wore only on Mount Olympus, and laid them to rest in chests of willow wood. Then gradually he transformed the king of the gods into a handsome mortal prince.

A Godling Comes to Earth

Once Hermes had finished, he took out his lyre and sang of Semele, while Zeus sat peacefully on his awesome throne, pleased with Olympus, with the gods, with the earth, with the mortals, with Hermes and with the little Theban princess.

All was not well, however, in the other chambers of the palace, for one goddess was very displeased. This goddess was Hera, Zeus's queen. She had lingered in the corridor when she saw Hermes streaking into the throne room and, upon hearing the words within, her face had twisted with wrath.

As a young goddess, she had been called Hera of the golden sandals, and she had ruled happily with her husband, Zeus. Then one day Strife had thrown a golden apple among the guests at a wedding feast, crying out in a loud voice: "This apple is for the most beautiful goddess. Whoever catches it will judge them."

Hermes told Zeus that when he caught it, the apple was so hot that it had burned his fingers, and because of this he had dropped it into the lap of a mortal. This mortal later judged the goddesses on the slopes of a mountain on earth, and he gave the apple not to Hera but to the goddess of love, Aphrodite.

Hera was heartbroken over the outcome of that contest. In the mansions of the gods, the whiteness of her arms and the smoothness of her shoulders had been greatly praised. Yet if a mortal had judged her second, or even third, what of her lord Zeus? She fled to Mount Olympus for reassurance. Alas! Zeus had just left for earth.

That night Zeus returned to Olympus, only to be

The Spirit of Spring

greeted with a thousand questions. Did he love her? Was she not more beautiful than the goddess of love? Why did he go to earth so often? Each night Hera continued to ask such things, until finally Zeus became furious.

Soon the other gods and goddesses, banqueting in their palaces on Mount Olympus, began ordering their musicians to play louder when Hera's cries and shrieks filled the evening air. Mortals also sighed when the gentle breezes of late afternoon flared up into potboiled and harassed gusts because of the wrath on high. The more Hera raged at Zeus to stay on Olympus, the more he left, until finally the enormous Olympian palace became still and deserted except for its lonely queen. Night would hear her screaming at her lord. Daylight would see her weeping over his departure and gazing miserably at the gaiety on earth below.

Jealousy of anyone who even spoke to Zeus began to grow within her. It did not diminish in the months that passed, but turned slowly into patient cunning and gave her the strength to stand long hours concealed behind columns in order that she might hear his plans. . . . Now she was doing just that to learn about Semele.

By the early hours of the morning, Hera knew everything. She stole off through the corridors to her chamber and there devised a plan.

She drew out a chest and pored over its contents. Lovingly she handled the evil knickknacks. There were disguises with which to fool men, vials of liquid to drive them mad, and drooping herbs with other uses. As she gazed at her hoard, a glow of pleasure came over her face and brought a shine to her marblelike skin.

A Godling Comes to Earth

While Hermes sang and Zeus dreamed, Hera stalked around her chamber disguising herself for the next day. She rubbed bark on her white and glistening cheeks. She tangled her hair. Then she pulled over her shoulders a tattered dress she had found on earth. That morning, horribly disguised, she left her chamber and crept into the deserted throne room.

She sat on the throne and stared down at the Theban land. She saw Semele with her golden hair like a sea, curling around the island of her small oval face. The girl was asleep, dreaming of the day when suitors would stream to her father begging her hand in marriage. Then, as if this sight were not enough, Hera saw Zeus descend to earth a small distance from the palace of King Cadmus. Her unsmiling eyes followed him as he washed the wisps of cloud dust from his face in a clear stream and proceeded through the royal gates of the city only to be lost from view within its towering walls.

Hera screamed an imprecation and, mounting a yellow cloud, followed him to Thebes.

Hera came to rest beside the servants' quarters. She had not stopped to wash her face. The dirtier she was the less the risk of being recognized as a goddess. She entered the kitchens and settled by the hearth. There she crouched, blending with the dark pots and listening to the servants gossip. They gradually became used to her bent figure, and the word passed through the kitchens that she was the barbarian slave, Beroe, who had been bought by the king from wandering traders.

The Spirit of Spring

When Hera heard this she was exceedingly pleased and began chattering with all who ventured near the hearth. That whole day she boasted of her hairdressing skills to anyone who would listen. She talked so much that in the evening the queen summoned her to arrange her daughter's hair for a banquet.

Hera hurried into Semele's chamber and almost grabbed at the golden head of hair. She combed the tresses with long strokes, while the young girl stared fascinated into a bronze mirror.

Hera held each lock up to the light, and as the sun sank beyond the horizon, she murmured, "It does not matter, for you shine like a torch."

Then she stood back, pretending to admire Semele's beauty.

"Now is the time, my dear, for you to have a husband," she whispered.

"I have already fallen in love," said Semele.

"Recently?"

"This morning."

"With a Theban lord?"

"With Zeus himself," Semele replied dreamily.

At this, Hera let out a hideous laugh, which would have frightened Semele to tears had she been listening to her servant instead of looking out the window at the heavens.

"My dear, princesses are easily fooled. It is undoubtedly some shepherd's son who is deceiving you with such nonsense."

"You are only jealous," retorted Semele, "because you must always comb the hair of others."

A Godling Comes to Earth

"No," Hera shook her head, "in time you will find out his heritage, when you are taken to his lowly hut."

With this remark, Hera stopped taunting Semele lest the Theban princess fly into a rage and order her from the chamber before she had accomplished her purpose.

"Don't listen to me," she sighed. "I am an old woman who knows life only by what she has overheard, sitting by the hearth. However, if your love is divine, why not tell him when he comes tomorrow to honor your beauty, which shines like that of an immortal. Ask him to appear to you not as he does to other mortals, but as he does to the goddesses—to Athena and, my dear, to Hera—in all his terrific splendors. Then you will know for sure if he is Zeus. Make him swear to do this. Yes! Make him swear by the river Styx, which flows through the underworld, an oath that neither gods nor men may break, to grant you what you ask. And should he do so, you will have proved old Beroe wrong."

Having uttered these words, Hera bowed and limped out, knowing well that the next day Semele would beg just such a favor from Zeus. The little princess was holding the bronze mirror up to her face at many different angles, smiling into it, then frowning, to glimpse the effect.

Hera went down the staircase and left the palace. She was impatient to return to Olympus and, having accomplished her evil design, half-flew, half-ran down the dark streets of Thebes and out its gates, rejoicing. At the stream where Zeus had stopped, she slipped off her rags, washed in its gentle water and soared to

Olympus. There she laughed until she cried, and her tears fell as evil rain upon the countryside below.

Dawn rose the next morning to find Zeus at the threshold of the Theban palace, awaiting his second audience with Semele. A trusted servant of King Cadmus ushered him into the throne room, and there the princess Semele greeted him. Zeus dropped back a step.

She was even more beautiful today than yesterday, and he fell mute gazing upon such perfection. She wore a dark-blue chiton and over this a brightly colored cloak, which was fastened at her right shoulder with a brilliant gem. Although her chiton was straight and simple, her cloak was magnificent. It had been woven into a pattern of blue spirals, red triangles and green dots, and along its borders were silvery stars mingled with archers and bears, seagoats and whales, flying steeds and scorpions. Her hair was arranged high upon her head, and tiny blue ribbons rippled here and there through its yellow waves.

Semele sat down on the throne and bade Zeus take the throne to her right. There, in front of a huge tapestry covered with purple sphinxes, the two talked on many subjects. Zeus spoke to her of geography, of Ethiopia (one of his favorite subjects, for he thought those peoples wondrous cooks judging from the delicious smell of their sacrifices) and of the deeds of the immortal gods.

Semele laughed. She teased. She told him tales. She listened and she bided her time. Then, with Zeus lost in wonder at her brilliance, she suddenly begged a favor.

Zeus, enraptured by her, replied immediately. "Of course! What shall it be? A dwarf from Punt to sing for

A Godling Comes to Earth

14 you? Two ibexes from Luristan to dance for you? Or a griffin with ivory wings to bear you high above the eastern lands, beyond the rich trading posts of Assur?"

"No," pouted Semele, and her face gleamed with the youthful vanity that Hera had discovered and preyed upon. "Swear by the eternal river Styx, which flows through the underworld, an oath that neither gods nor men can break, to grant me what I ask."

Zeus, seeing the little princess perched daintily on the big Theban throne, was powerless. He fell to the level of a mortal. He had no strength whatsoever. Now it was only important that he remove the frown from his loved one's face. He swore the oath without thinking.

"Show me yourself as you are—as king of the gods," said Semele. "Clothe yourself in all your splendors and appear before me next as you do before Athena, and also Hera."

"Semele, you don't know what you ask."

"If you love me. . . ."

"Child! I forbid you. Ask something else immediately."

Semele only stared hard at the figure-eight shields that the court artist had painted on the wall opposite the thrones to remind the Thebans of their stubborn valor in past battles.

"You promised me my favor. If you love me. . . ."

"But Semele, it is because of this that I beg you to change your wish." He interrupted her quickly.

"I will do nothing of the sort." Semele refused to talk further and rose to go.

"You have asked a terrible thing," Zeus spoke sadly as he left the court for Olympus.

The Spirit of Spring

Zeus arrived on Mount Olympus a few minutes later and went straight to his palace. He entered his chamber and began to take out his splendors which Hermes had laid away in the willow wood chests. The sunrays sizzled and spat as he brought them forth.

"Quiet!" Zeus snapped and shook them. The sunrays were the most powerful of all (excluding the thunderbolt) and covered him with such hot fire that neither the snow nor the rain could put it out.

Next he pulled out lightning, and after that snow, hail and ice. One hailstone escaped and hit him hard on the wrist. He held it with his other hand and thought of Semele.

"Oh, Semele," he murmured. "How could you have asked for these?"

Then he shook out his great chilly mists and lonely clouds. Zeus grew more and more somber as he arrayed himself in the trappings of the king of the gods.

Suddenly he exclaimed, "Where is it?" and brightened when he thought he had lost his torrent of rain. "Where has it gone?"

"Oh," he sighed. It was lying under the tornado.

Zeus finally finished. Holding his breath, not daring to look lest he break the oath he had made to Semele, he drew his long, black thunderbolt out of its giant scabbard. With this in his hand, he set forth from Olympus. Although he had donned his lighter splendors—those that the one-eyed giants had made for him long ago—he was a fearsome sight. All the gods and goddesses turned around. The sun stood still and gazed upon him as though it were looking in a mirror at its own awful, blazing beauty.

A Godling Comes to Earth

16   While Zeus was preparing himself on Olympus, Semele waited impatiently at Thebes. She could not stay seated at her loom. She slipped out of the palace and wandered off to the stream by the walls of the city. The princess sat down and leaned against a tree, and while her eyes watched the sky, her fingers nervously twined little flowers into a wreath to wear for the occasion.

Finally, she caught sight of a speck in the heavens, which glowed even then. It was coming closer. She stood up to watch. It was now the size of one of the stars. She had no need to strain her eyes. It was becoming larger by the second. The speck grew and grew until it was the size of the sun on a cloudy day, and then the size of the sun on a bright day, and still it did not stop. It mushroomed into the orange sun of a summer sunset, and at this point Semele clapped her hands for joy, for she could just make out the form of Zeus. But her hands stopped quickly, for she was beginning to feel uncommonly warm. She felt hot. She felt as though she were roasting like a piece of meat on a spit. Her arms flew up like the wings of a frightened bird, but there was no way she could escape.

The land became hotter and hotter and hotter. The Theban air grew white with the heat, and Semele began to shriek in anguish. She cried to Zeus to go, to break his oath if he loved her. But he could not do this, even for her, since oaths are stronger than either gods or men. And so, with one last plea on her lips and one last, "If you love me . . ." she died. Before Zeus had even stepped onto the earth, her small frame had shattered from the heat.

Zeus mourned when he saw her, as what had been so certain, so alive, was now so broken and so still. The

The Spirit of Spring

earth seemed to mourn with him for its own. Even
Hera, who had watched the scene with great glee from
Olympus, fell back on her couch limp with fatigue once
the deed was accomplished.

Zeus eased himself down on a rock and was deep
in thought when suddenly he caught sight of something
moving where Semele had once stood. He looked closer.
There was a gurgle and he could vaguely make out the
form of a baby boy. Shoots of ivy and white flowers
had curled about him to form a cradle.

Zeus picked him up and held him gently. The child,
being immortal, had not been harmed by his splendors. In fact, he clutched at the sunrays on Zeus's mantle and burbled because their brilliance pleased him.
Zeus was amazed and put him down, so that the child
could play with one of the tinier bolts of lightning.
Watching him, the king of the gods smiled. There and
then he named his son. Forever, by gods and men, he
would be known as Dionysos, son of Zeus, Child of
the Great Light.

At this, Zeus felt an intimation of danger for his
son. The events of the past afternoon suddenly seemed
too evil. It was as though another power had plotted
against him, had succeeded, and had destroyed his
Semele. The child must be concealed immediately.
Scooping up Dionysos, Zeus stuffed the little one into
his thigh and bound him up with golden buckles made
of molded sunrays. Thereupon he flew straight to his
palace.

"My lord, you have split Thebes in two!" cried Hermes.
"Never have there been so many rumors. They say
that the princess Semele fell in love with a shepherd's

A Godling Comes to Earth

son and that you struck her down with your thunderbolt for saying he was Zeus. What happened, Zeus?"

Hermes had just escorted Semele to the underworld. The princess had been in a wretched state, had told him a garbled tale about a wicked servant and had cried endlessly while being rowed across the river Styx to the realm of the dead. Hermes had an idea who the wicked servant might have been, but he did not voice it.

"Why can't I find something to look at?" Zeus complained, disregarding Hermes' question. The king of the gods was gazing moodily out the window upon the earth, hoping to be diverted, but his eyes kept landing on Thebes. "Why can't the amber route interest me—the ivory route, or the gold route. And where is that confounded squawking coming from?"

He rose from his throne and looked underneath. There was another squeal. He looked under his footstool, while Hermes peered behind a column.

"I think, Zeus, though I am probably wrong, that it is coming from you."

"From me? I beg your pardon, Hermes."

Zeus suddenly realized that Hermes was not being rude, but that the crying actually was coming from himself. He listened to what was now a hefty bellow, turned red and remembered his child.

"Hermes, I forgot to tell you. I have a son."

"Congratulations!" Hermes always felt elated whenever an entry was made into life.

"Thank you, Hermes, but what shall I do with it?" Zeus murmured.

"Keep it from the queen of the gods!" Hermes exclaimed and he told Zeus the terrible tale of Hera's treachery.

"Poor Semele!" moaned Zeus when the messenger had finished the tale. "What mortal on earth could hope to be a match for Hera."

"Zeus," said Hermes, who was now very concerned for the child. "I will take the infant to Ino, one of Semele's sisters, who is still loyal to her. The boy will live in a Theban palace and grow up with Theban princes. Ino's two sons, Melikertes and Learchos, will be his playmates. He will be like a mortal. . . ."

"What?" interrupted Zeus. "My son like a mortal? Dionysos will never be like a mortal, no matter where he grows up."

He unbuckled his thigh and held up his little boy to Hermes.

"This is Dionysos," he said, "the son of Zeus and Semele."

Then he sighed, "She was so young, Hermes."

Fleetingly, Zeus wondered how words or music could ever hope to capture the beauty of the Theban princess as she had stood before him in the throne room of her father's palace.

The infant started to cry.

"He wants his mother, Zeus," said Hermes gently. Taking the infant into his arms, Zeus's messenger could only bear him away to a stepmother in Thebes.

After Hermes had taken his leave, Zeus suddenly noticed that the palace was unusually still, and he wondered where Hera was. He searched for her in every chamber, only to discover from Iris, her messenger,

A Godling Comes to Earth

that she had left for Thebes on a very urgent matter.

"What matter?" thundered Zeus.

"I don't know," quavered Iris, fingering the folds of her many-colored chiton—she was the goddess of the rainbow.

"Dionysos!" exclaimed Zeus.

Zeus tore after the queen of the gods and met Hermes in the air midway between earth and heaven, the wings on his sandals flapping madly.

"Zeus! You have no idea what she has done—she overheard our plans for Dionysos. Hera has driven Ino and her husband mad! They're both trying to kill their children."

"Yes. But my son! Where is he?"

"In the palace of King Cadmus!"

"You left him there! Go back immediately and look after him."

They flew to earth. Hermes sped to the palace and Zeus rushed to attend to the uproar outside. As he approached, he could hear Hera shrieking, "That's right, Athamas. Your son is a deer. Shoot him! Quickly!"

Zeus appeared a few moments later. He chased Hera to the other side of the grove. There Semele's sister, Ino, was frantically chopping wood in order to kindle a blazing fire and boil the other child, Melikertes. To aid her, Hera had produced a huge cauldron and was screaming, "Here you are! Find some firewood!"

Hera was in a frenzy of wickedness. She had never pushed herself so hard, nor tormented one family so much.

Zeus finally caught up with her, and he would have brought peace to the grove had not Hera seen him coming and cast a new spell over Ino. Now Ino thought that Zeus was feeding that blaze and that Zeus intended to boil her son. She spat at him, grabbed her little boy and began to run. She ran and ran, and only when she reached the cliffs along the sea did she pause. Then, with one last look behind, she and her son vanished over the crags and into the foaming water below.

Zeus, approaching the bluffs, thought of Semele and how he had been unable to help her, but now he was not bound by an oath. He spoke his wish and changed both Ino and Melikertes into immortals.

"Henceforth you, Ino, will be Leucothea, the white goddess of the sea, and you, Melikertes, will be Palaimon, the guardian of mariners."

As the king of the gods spoke, the sea smoothed out its ripples, and with its surface calm and majestic, rose to welcome Semele's sister and her son into the bright company of underwater deities.

Hera ran up. In a rage at Zeus's intervention, she turned all the Theban women into seabirds. They unfurled their wings clumsily and bumped into each other in confusion, but finally managed to soar. Then they sighted Ino and Melikertes, now Leucothea and Palaimon, and flew to them, shrilling in their new language.

The mother and son were riding triumphantly through the waves in a chariot driven by Poseidon, the god of the sea. They were off to the Isthmus.

The sea held its breath in order not to disturb the deities who were traveling its paths for the first time. In a short while the blue water would be romping playfully beside them as Palaimon exercised his stable of finny creatures in the morning and Leucothea visited

A Godling Comes to Earth

other sea nymphs in the afternoon. But now it was courteous and held back so as not to disturb the pageant. Leucothea, Poseidon, and Palaimon rode away, while a circle of pure white seabirds swooped high, swooped low, but kept always above them.

Even Hera could not help being affected by the beauty of the sight on the waves. While she was watching, unable to take her eyes from the procession, Zeus had hurried back to the palace.

Hermes came to the threshold of the palace with the godling in his arms and looked around the grove in disbelief. He had no idea the destruction had been so terrible. Whole trees had been uprooted. The remains of blazing fires were still smouldering here and there. Arrows stuck in tree trunks and in the ground. Enormous cauldrons were overturned and boiling water was pouring out. The child had to go—quickly. He must be hidden.

Zeus gave the command, "To the gardens of Nysa, Hermes," and kissed the infant farewell.

As Hermes turned, he felt in his arms four legs instead of two, and looking down he saw with astonishment a kid, which stretched its neck and began to eat his hat. Zeus had transformed the baby completely. Only thus would Hermes and Dionysos be safe from Hera as they traveled the long road before them to the magical gardens of Nysa. There Dionysos would grow up far, far from his native Thebes.

Hera was enraged. The baby had escaped. She burned to locate Nysa. She asked every god she could find where these gardens were situated, but each one named a different place—Arabia, Ethiopia, Egypt, Babylon, the Red Sea, Thrace, Thessaly, India, Macedon, Naxos—until the whole of the world had been named and she knew no more than when she had begun. One thing she did know as she staggered back to her chamber: when the child left Nysa, there would be nowhere, *nowhere* in the realm of gods or men, where he would escape her wrath.

A Godling Comes to Earth

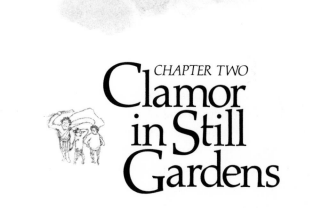

CHAPTER TWO
Clamor in Still Gardens

*Dionysos squinted to make sure. Suddenly, at the
top of the tree his five nurses appeared in a row.*

*H*ERMES BORE DIONYSOS OFF TO MAGICAL GARDENS where lawns of parsley and violets, forests of richly scented Cypress trees, green groves and ringing brooks formed an unmapped paradise, a fragrant and ever-blooming, a spacious and ever-expanding nursery for a bursting, broadening baby god.

Changing Dionysos back into a baby, Hermes sat him on a hillside overlooking a wide valley. Even after Hermes had gone, Dionysos remained in this upright position, balanced by the thickness of his swaddling clothes. Only his small face was visible through the thick folds, and his bright eyes stared unblinkingly into the vista opening before them. He had been alone but a second before his nurses arrived.

"There he is!" one shrilled and waved to the others.

They rushed down upon him, slipping and sliding on the luxuriant vines.

"Dionysos . . ." another hallooed.

They scooped him up immediately and kissed

The Spirit of Spring

him, clucking their tongues as they passed him between them and shedding a few tears as they discussed his mother's dire fate.

"What a terrible thing . . ." the first sniffed.

"To be born from one's father's thigh . . ." lamented the second.

"Oh . . ." all five wailed as they hugged him again.

The nurses were the Hyades. They had never looked after a child before, for they were the unmarried daughters of Atlas, the giant who held the heavens on his head. Their names were Filtered Light, Crow, Famous, Dim and Generous. Zeus had just asked them to bring up Dionysos.

In the beginning, when the baby could only move a few feet on hands and knees, everything went smoothly. As the godling grew older, however, his legs strengthened, and his stride, though still a child's stride, was long enough and swift enough to leave his tottering nurses, who unfortunately were lame, far behind.

"Dionysos!" they called.

No longer were they able to hobble beside him and explore the Nysian gardens with him, laughing and gathering honey.

"Dionysos!" they began to call more frantically.

No longer were they able to halt every hour and sink down into a cool woodland dell to sip a potion of spruce juice with a sprig of ivy in it.

"Dionysos! Dionysos! Dionysos!"

Soon Filtered Light, Crow, Famous, Dim and Generous were spending their mornings and afternoons dragging their lame bodies up to the peaks of silver fir trees. There, high above the earth, they tried to find

Clamor in Still Gardens

their charge. Anxiously they scanned the well-known paths and their eyes pierced the thick foliage, hoping underneath to spot a shock of thick, black hair, a flash of bright purple mantle, or a glimmer from golden sandals.

"Why can't he stay near our dwelling?" cried Crow from the treetops.

"Perhaps he should have some toys!" exclaimed Generous from a cliff.

"Toys!" echoed Dim elatedly, swaying on a bush. "That's what the child needs. . . ."

"But there are no toys in Nysa," faltered Famous. "No clay apples, no wooden goats."

"Then we'll bring him live ones."

"Yes!" chimed in everyone.

The nurses slid from the trees and cliffs to the ground, or rather they toppled down, and picking themselves out of the prickly bushes into which they inevitably fell, they wobbled away through the gardens.

Shortly afterwards, Hermes returned, eager to see the divine infant. It had been difficult for him to find the Nysian gardens again, for they were enchanted and were held apart from the world by magical spells that made it almost impossible for anyone to locate them twice. However, after a certain amount of spying and swooping, hovering and diving—sometimes into the wrong garden—Hermes had managed to land to the side of the high-ceilinged cave that was Dionysos' Nysian home. Clutching a rattle firmly under his arm, he crossed the threshold to find the cradle.

Failing in his attempt, Hermes went back again and

The Spirit of Spring

set out through the gardens. Suddenly he felt something tugging at one of the wings on his sandals. He whirled around and dropped the rattle in astonishment when he saw Dionysos. The baby he had expected was no longer an infant but was a sturdy child, with black hair tumbling all over his forehead. He was seated in the middle of a pile of green vines, which he was happily untangling.

"Who are you?" asked the child.

"I am Hermes," replied the messenger, aghast.

Hermes had a theory that if a god did not achieve greatness by the time he was one day old, left on his own, he might never achieve it at all. And, seeing Dionysos for the first time, Hermes was concerned in case this particular son of Zeus turn into a complete peasant and run wild and unkempt for the rest of his days through Nysa.

"I have something to say to you." Hermes cleared his throat. "I am going to tell you about your family."

This statement had a magical effect. Hermes had never seen such an expression of delight on anyone's face.

"A story," breathed the little boy.

"It isn't a story, exactly," said Hermes with embarrassment, for he had no intention of telling the story that concerned Zeus and Semele. He was only going to give Dionysos a short geography lesson, as Zeus had directed, to imbue him with the proper sense of his city and his mortal lineage.

"Thebes," Hermes began, sitting down beside Dionysos, "Thebes is a wealthy city in Greece. It has seven gates and is built around a hill. While the houses of the townspeople stretch out below, the hill is occupied by great temples and royal mansions, that of your grandfather Cadmus being foremost in splendor. . . ."

"My grandfather?" asked the little boy.

"Yes, he is the king and lives with your grandmother Harmonia in a magnificent palace."

Suddenly all five of the Hyades tumbled into the clearing, whirling vines, driving before them a herd of kids, heifers, and delicately spotted fawns, which lowered their baffled heads and shied away from the seated god and godling, then charged forward spurred on by the nurses and buried their soft muzzles in Dionysos' lap.

"Dionysos! Dionysos!" the Hyades shrieked, picking themselves up, not even noticing the messenger of the gods who was hidden under the multitude of affectionate and eager baby animals. "Dionysos! Look at your toys. . . ."

With that, Generous tripped over Hermes' rattle. Her arms flung open and presents rained down over the heads and shoulders of the godling, who was delighted, and Hermes, who could not have been more disconcerted. Red apples, ripe figs, sesame seeds, pine cones, peaches, ears of corn, bunches of violets, asphodels and roses sailed down the folds of both their cloaks, caught in Hermes' hat, and then were tossed around by the wagging tails and pitching horns of the animals.

"Who would give such things to a god?" exclaimed Hermes.

He leapt to his feet.

The Spirit of Spring

"A god!" gasped Dionysos. The little boy had been flattened by the animals' charge, and the creatures were all standing over him, their tiny horns lowered with interest, for he was exactly their own age.

Hermes was already in the air, circling over the confusion on the ground. He looked once more in disbelief and then disappeared out of sight in the direction of Mount Olympus.

"Your son is an extremely lively godling," Hermes finished his report to Zeus later over a cup of nectar, "but I really feel he should have a boy or two in Nysa with him for company. I would send Pan at once. . . ."

"Dionysos has his nurses."

"They're lame, Zeus," said Hermes, and added hesitantly, "and very bizarre. While I was there, they showered him with fruits and flowers and let loose a herd of animals for him to play with."

"But Pan . . ." Zeus shook his head.

"Zeus," said Hermes, "Dionysos is old enough now to learn something useful about the woodlands and meadows around him—and who but my son could teach him?"

"Perhaps that sprite Silenos," said Zeus thoughtfully.

"Silenos!" Hermes looked horrified and put down his cup. "Why, he's just as bad as . . ."

Hermes caught himself and said instead, pleadingly, "Remember, Zeus, I loved a nymph called Drope, and she bore me a son. Remember how hard you laughed and how hard the rest of the gods laughed when he peeped up at them out of his rabbitskins, with his pointed ears and horns. That is why I, that is we, named him Pan, which means *all*, because he delighted all our hearts."

Hermes paused just long enough for Zeus to smile, and then hurried on. "But your mother, Rhea, wouldn't let him onto Mount Olympus. She said he was too ugly. And so he roamed the earth below, an eternal child, looking always for playmates."

"But he found them, Hermes."

"The shepherds? No, Zeus. He was their god and the god of their flocks. The immortal gods, they were his brothers, his uncles, and his cousins and his aunts, and should have been his playmates. But what did they do? They laughed at his simplicity and his gaiety; they forbade him a palace on Olympus and his uncle Apollo even wheedled the art of prophecy from him!"

"That may be true, Hermes, but I still can't see Pan as a tutor. . . ."

"Then why couldn't he be a playmate?"

Zeus turned to his messenger.

Hermes said hurriedly, "Are you going to let Dionysos grow up in Nysa with five eccentric nurses, who are also lame, and Silenos, who is as old as the mountains from which he comes, and no playmate?"

Zeus hesitated.

"With no one his own age?"

Zeus reconsidered. It was just this question that led him to send Pan—goatish, wistful Pan—along with Silenos to join Dionysos in Nysa.

The next day Dionysos noticed a commotion in a quiet mountain pool. He saw the forms of frightened water

The Spirit of Spring

nymphs fleeing downstream. There were a series of
gushings and gurglings, and a creature heaved himself
out of the water and stood upright on the bank.

"My name is Silenos," said he.

He was a strange figure. While the upper part of
his body was that of an elderly, corpulent man, the
lower part was that of a beast. His legs were so shaggy
and bow-shaped that they could only be those of a—
"Yes," thought the little god, "a goat! And he has
hooves and horns and a tail to match! But what is he?"

"I am a water sprite," said Silenos, reading his expression.

Dionysos was speechless. Hitherto he had en-
visioned a world filled with female nurses who could
not run, and when they tried, tripped over the endless
material of their flowing chitons and began to weep.

He had met some water sprites in his ramblings,
but they had behaved exactly like his nurses. They
dressed in the same flimsy, billowing robes and had
wasted his time by combing their hair before they would
play with him, after they had finished playing with him
and even during the game. All they ever wanted to
do was to stay in the reeds. They made a great fuss
about leaving the water and kept explaining that they
might lose their stream. In all, they were as unskilled
in his favorite sports as the Hyades, and on top of
that he had grown too large for theirs. Dionysos could
no longer conceal himself behind a reed. The day before, he had begged them to join him in a swimming
race.

"Too tiring," they murmured, "too tiring," and
they continued sunning themselves on the rocks.

Clamor in Still Gardens

Now that he might have a new playmate, Dionysos looked with interest at Silenos.

"There are many more of me," Silenos rumbled. "Sileni, we're called. But I'm the best and the greatest and the biggest and the wisest of us all!"

Suddenly Dionysos longed to know more about the woods and the brooks that harbored such unknown beings. Silenos could not have been born in Nysa. He must have come from another garden, another brook, and somewhere outside the Nysian gardens were more like him.

The little god was so thrilled with his latest visitor that he acted as courteously as he knew how. He brushed the waterdrops from his guest's long beard. When he straightened up, he found a similar though smaller creature standing near them. This one had just come out from behind a tree and stood shyly (for the moment) to the side, waiting to be introduced.

"Are you a water sprite, too?" asked Dionysos politely.

"I am not, you black-haired fledgling! I'm Pan!" this one said.

Dionysos looked him over carefully and saw that he, too, was half-man, half-beast. Instead of a round, bald head, however, he had an abundance of curly hair, which fell over his forehead and around his pointed ears, setting the stage for a devilish mouth, a snub-nose and two roving blue eyes. His hands seemed to twitch with perpetual excitement and eagerness, and they held a strange set of pipes.

Pan suddenly turned, did a jig and finished answering Dionysos' question.

The Spirit of Spring

"I don't like the water. I wouldn't go near it at all if it weren't for the nymphs. . . ."

He had been standing by the pool when he said this, and before Dionysos knew what was happening, the newcomer had caught a naiad by her ankle and flipped her out of the water like a fish.

"It is Pan!" shouted Silenos above the shrieks and screams of the water nymph.

"Silenos, you old mountain goat!" cried the other, tossing the naiad back into her stream.

What followed was the boisterous joy of two woodland deities meeting each other after months, perhaps years, of living on different mountains or in different meadows. The forest folk had excessive pride, however, and this forbade them ever to admit elation at such meetings, and prompted them to couch their pleasure in the most unflattering greetings imaginable.

"Are you a god, too?" Pan asked Dionysos after he had finished with Silenos.

"I guess not, if you're one." Dionysos felt his head forlornly for signs of horns.

"It's true we can't all be gods. I only thought Zeus would have given me just one god as a comrade after all these years with no one to play with but those Arcadian shepherds!" moaned Pan disconsolately.

There was silence. Now that the three had been introduced, they stood eyeing one another. Each was wondering what to do next, but Pan never wondered long and he never let a silence go unbroken. After giving Silenos' ear a playful yank, he sprang agilely to the other side of the pool.

There he paused. Leaning his back against a tree

Clamor in Still Gardens

trunk and crossing his cloven hooves delicately, he put his pipes to his lips and began to play the most beautiful strain that had ever sounded in the Nysian gardens. So sweetly did it come upon the grove that even Silenos sat down and sat still.

A nymph ventured out on her rock, then another and another until all the water sprites had ceased to tremble over the newcomer and had lined up on their hard, stone perches in the middle of the pool, now front-row seats for Pan's performance.

Something new had arrived in the gardens, not only something to be seen but something to be heard. The ears of the wild things had caught the tidings. It would be a long time before the proud grasses by the mountain stream forgot their matted state after that host of forest listeners surged over them and settled upon them, struggling for a better view of the player.

Dionysos lay back against a tree, and in the enchantment of the melody his eyes became pensive. At the first notes of Pan's pipes, the rabbits and the foxes had crept around him, surfacing here and there from the black depths of the forest. The furry creatures curled up in his lap and in the hollows of his folded arms.

Pan had collected all the sounds of the wild earth, and with his fingers he was channeling them through the thin reeds of his pipes. The forest was enraptured. Each being listened to a harmony of himself singing with the universe, a harmony impossible for one singer to hear when he sings in the vast chorus.

The melody drew gently to a close and Dionysos was left in the stillness of the grove with an overpower-

The Spirit of Spring

ing yearning to visit that land, from which the song came, beyond the gardens of Nysa.

As Dionysos grew older his bearing assumed new dignity. He was no longer the chunky godling Hermes had visited that sunny morning when the Hyades had interrupted his geography lesson. Now he was a powerful youth accompanied by an enthusiastic band—Pan, Silenos, the Hyades and all the animals—in his ramblings through the orchards, fields and flower beds he had planted from the toys given him by his nurses.

"Look what I made!" Dionysos cried one day as he waved a staff twined with ivy and myrtle. "It's for our excursions. I've named it a thyrsus. See if you can make one, too!"

Pan dived into the undergrowth and came back a few minutes later clasping a staff wreathed with so many vines and flowers that he could hardly carry it.

"No!" said Silenos. "Look at mine."

Silenos had wreathed his with grapevines, and the corpulent sprite was now holding it above his head, eating the grapes.

"Look at ours!" cried the Hyades breathlessly.

Each one of them had attached a pine cone to a staff's tip. Now they were limping around Dionysos, flinging up their thyrsi in delight. Silenos joined in with his. Pan did also, and tried to play his pipes at the same time.

As soon as they had all collapsed on the ground, Dionysos said, "I've made something else, too."

He produced seven high-handled cups of ivy wood.

"What are those for?" growled Pan. The sprite

Clamor in Still Gardens

sprang to his hooves belligerently to peer at the cups, for he had done nothing all day except whisper "drought" in the ear of a sleeping water nymph, scaring her out of her dewy dreams and back into the wrong stream.

"They're wonderful!" exclaimed Silenos. "No more clumsy horns to drink from. . . ."

With that, he struck a rock with his staff and a stream of milk came out for refreshment.

"No, Silenos!" cried Dionysos. "The cup's not for milk, it's for wine."

He swung around to Pan.

"I made it for you," he said. "You know how much you've been complaining lately about the goats' horns. . . ."

As soon as Pan understood that the high-handled cups with the sturdy bases had been invented for him, he accepted one. He held his quizzically, since he was not quite sure what to do with it. Before he could throw it to the ground and protest that such things were fit only for peasants sitting around tables in cottages and not for sprites who roved in the wild and gods like himself, Silenos had filled it with sparkling wine, which he poured from a goatskin. Then he proceeded to serve the others.

They raised their cups thirstily and downed their draughts in a gulp.

This drink was the miracle of Nysa. Long ago a drop of ichor, the blood that flows in the gods' veins, fell from Mount Olympus onto the earth below. It took root, spread rapidly and blossomed into a luxuriant creeper with brilliant purple fruit, which later became known as a grapevine. While still a child, Dionysos found it and discovered the uses of its berries, which could be eaten by themselves or pressed into an exhilarating liquid called wine. With Silenos and Pan, he had set about cultivating these wild grapevines. Now they were arranged over the countryside of Nysa in such neat rows that even the Hyades could stroll through them without tripping and the vines produced regularly a harvest of sumptuous grapes.

"Sometimes I would like to stay in Nysa forever," said Pan, draining his winecup and contentedly twirling Dionysos' new invention around his finger. "And other times . . ."

Pan did not finish his sentence. Instead he took up his pipes and let his fingers glide over the reeds, and the whole woodland idled.

"And other times," he mused, upon reaching the final note, "I miss Arcadia. . . ."

Dionysos was lost in thought. Through Silenos' teachings he was well versed in the lore of every aspect of forest and meadow, and his love and concern for all growing things had taken him to the outskirts of Nysa. Now that these far parts were cultivated, however, he looked more and more longingly to the realms beyond, which still were knotted and tangled.

"I would like to go out," the young god murmured.

"Why?" asked Pan. "You don't have any land of your own."

"To cultivate the wild vines. To discover if we can make things grow there as well as we do here. To see your land. . . ."

Clamor in Still Gardens

Pan cocked his horns. So did Silenos.

"Maybe we should go out for a quick visit to do these things," Pan suggested, "and then come back to Nysa."

"Would you like that?" asked Dionysos excitedly.

"Of course!" Pan and Silenos nodded together.

They all snatched up their thyrsi and winecups, and mounting the Hyades on the backs of goats and donkeys, they raced back to the cave for a feast during which they would lay their plans.

The next morning the three arose early. The Hyades garlanded their thyrsi with fresh flowers and vines and gave Dionysos as a going-away present a hat with two horns on it that resembled a helmet.

Pan, Silenos and all the kids, goats, heifers and fawns gazed at him with surprise when he put the hat on shyly.

"Does this make me a god, Pan?" asked Dionysos.

"You certainly look the way you should look," Pan exclaimed.

"Like us!" agreed Silenos.

They bade the Hyades good-bye and set out eagerly for the Nysian gates, which opened to the world beyond. At the border they looked back over the fragrant land of Nysa. In the distance the broad forests spread over the hills.

Dionysos sighed and then paused; he blinked once, a second time. It was a windless day, but the uppermost branches of one of the fir trees were thrashing frantically. Someone was climbing them. It couldn't be! He peered steadily for a moment. Oh, no! He squinted once more to make sure. It was! Suddenly, at the top of the tree, his five nurses appeared in a row. Although usually ill at ease off the ground, this time they were swaying on high, undaunted, swinging their winecups and waving their thyrsi back and forth with ardor terrifying to the upturned gaze of the departing trio.

"Farewell! Farewell!" they cried.

"The Hyades!" exclaimed Dionysos. "They're giving us a last farewell, but why from the highest tree in the forest? It makes me dizzy to look at the landscape."

"They're all going to fall," cried Silenos, horror-stricken, as he watched the wobbling forms.

"We're only going for a visit," shouted Dionysos to them.

"Madder than water nymphs," muttered Pan, and was rewarded for the comparison by a swat from a reed appearing out of a nearby stream.

"It's only for a visit . . ." shouted Dionysos, again.

"Farewell! Farewell! Farewell!"

Clamor in Still Gardens

CHAPTER THREE

The Coming of Spring

Dionysos, Pan and Silenos, wreathed with ivy and
laurel, stole into the villages of mortals by night.

*D*IONYSOS, PAN AND SILENOS, WREATHED WITH IVY AND laurel and holding their thyrsi, stole into the small villages of mortals by night, and together they pruned and watered the long, tangled grapevines.

"Look!" a farmer would shout in the morning. What had been wild and unkempt the day before was suddenly neat and cultivated. This was not all that would happen.

"The heat no longer comes through my walls," a woman exclaimed with delight by a village fountain. "I woke up this morning and found ivy all over the side of my house."

Rhea, the goddess of the earth, smiled at this remark, thinking of Zeus's birth. She remembered that hour so far back, when in the pain of child-bearing, she had gripped the ground with her fingers. The great god had been born, and from the imprint of her hand in the soil the five-pointed leaf of the ivy had appeared in celebration. However, while Zeus had continued to grow in power over the years, the little plant had been all but forgotten—until now. Now her grandson,

The Spirit of Spring

Dionysos, was planting it in villages, and soon it would adorn all homes, from the palaces of princes to the simple huts of shepherds.

"Figs!" the young men cried, coming upon an orchard of fig trees that had sprung up overnight in an unused meadow. "A miracle!"

"Asphodels," the girls sighed over the flowers and made wreaths of their blossoms. These were Pan's contributions—Pan, who however grumpy he was at first, always loved an adventure in the end, after others had finished the drudgery.

"They're to herald the spring," he had whispered to Dionysos by way of explanation, blushing hard to his horns lest Silenos hear and tease him.

The villagers began to feel the spirit of Dionysos rising in their planting and harvesting. They quickly learned how to make wine, taking the hints Dionysos put in the vineyards to explain the process: a basket filled with grapes, a giant vat in which to press the grapes and rows of amphoras to hold the juice.

"Who is he?" asked the villagers over and over, as they sat together in the evenings, sipping their new drink awkwardly out of bowls and pitchers and horns.

One night, after arranging the display, Dionysos forgot his winecup. A host of potters descended upon it in the morning. They worked all that day and all the next to make enough copies to satisfy the demands of the village.

"Could he be a mortal or is he a . . . a . . ."

Though the countryfolk did not yet dare call the youth they glimpsed in the woodlands a god, they talked of his parentage in whispers. Only an immortal had such gifts as wine to bestow upon weary mortals. The villagers reproduced his cup many times over, in many sizes and many colors, and considered these as sacred symbols of Dionysos. As the grapevines became more abundant and the wine more delicious, the men began to leave a winecup outside their cottages for this new protector, to honor him with the first juice of the harvest. This custom spread and gradually became a tradition, so that at harvest time a special high-handled cup would be taken down from the wall of every rustic's cottage, filled with wine and left outside in gratitude to Dionysos.

"Good," said Pan, drinking it all.

"Excellent," agreed Silenos, cornering the last drop in the goblet Pan had discarded. "I think this village is the best so far. . . ."

"Onward to the next," said Dionysos.

When Hera saw these cups dotting the country below, she flew down at once. She handled them grimly, and looking around at the luxuriant flowers and fruits and vines, she knew that Dionysos had come out—at last—from the magical gardens of Nysa.

"Here on a visit!" she whispered to herself, after listening to a muffled conference between three horned comrades in a thicket, too dense for her to penetrate.

"Now, where is he?" she muttered next, little knowing that Dionysos had his own set of horns and was one of the three.

"Wherever he is, I'll see it's more than a visit!" she cried, her voice rising to a shriek.

The Spirit of Spring

Exile
to the East

CHAPTER FOUR

*The sprig threw itself across the shooting stream
of water, unraveling, stretching forward.*

*I*T WAS A DREARY AFTERNOON ON EARTH. CLOUDS HUNG low; the bulging black ones were conducting an afternoon of unrest by hunching over the countryside, pretending at any moment to drop their burden of rain and dust. All morning Hermes had been fretting and fidgeting in Zeus's throne room on Mount Olympus about the uncertain weather below, wondering whether he could loop the world before it rained, or whether the rain would tumble around him in the middle, or whether it would even rain at all, or whether it would rain for days.

He paced back and forth, back and forth, the wings of his sandals nervously twitching, until Zeus could endure it no longer and ordered him from his presence. Stranded in the colonnaded hall, Hermes decided it was too late now to take a whirl in the paths of the sky. He decided instead to stand outside Hera's door, so he streaked off down the corridor, his spirits rising at the prospect of eavesdropping on the queen of the gods.

"Here on a visit," he could hear her muttering, as

The Spirit of Spring

she stalked around inside her chamber. "Here on a visit!"

Hera was violent on the subject of the flowers and vines that were sprouting and blooming in neat rows over the countryside.

"I shall bewitch him!" she cried in annoyance. "How could he think to escape my wrath by going back to Nysa! It is an insult to my power! He shall never see Nysa again. I will bewitch him and drive him away from his fruitful vineyards to the deserts of Egypt, the dry and parched lands of India and the burning wastes of Asia." There was a sinister pause. "And he'll never make anything grow!"

Hermes rushed back to the throne room.

"Hera's bewitching Dionysos," he announced. "She's sending him to the east!"

"She is!" cried Zeus.

"She certainly is," gasped Hermes and dropped down on Zeus's footstool.

"Hermes, I will . . ." Zeus began and stopped suddenly. He wondered what he could do. If he brought Dionysos to Mount Olympus now, his very existence would turn into a round of quarrels and jarring incidents such as the one that occurred long ago by the Theban palace. The king of the gods shuddered.

"Dionysos cannot come to Mount Olympus," he stated. "He is going to the east!"

"Not the east!" Hermes echoed.

"Hermes," Zeus commanded. "Go to the outskirts of Nysa. Prepare Dionysos for his coming travels. The queen of the gods is determined to harry him no matter where he goes on earth, but I cannot welcome

Exile to the East

him in my palace until the two of them have made their peace. Should I protect him now—even remotely—he would never grow into the mighty powers that have been set aside for him since his birth. Now, take him the challenge of the east!"

Hermes was already on his feet, ready to act as the god of all crossroads. But before he reached the towering threshold, he blurted out, "Dionysos mustn't go all the way to India alone. Send the sileni, too, Zeus!"

"The sileni!" Zeus echoed. "No!"

"I'll book a passage for Pan myself," pled Hermes, "but you must give the satyrs permission to go!"

"You're booking a passage for Pan! On what?"

"A moon-boat! It's a ship I'm acquiring for Dionysos —built on the lines of a new moon."

"What?"

"Zeus, it was you who made me the god of travelers."

"Such ideas are commendable, Hermes, but Dionysos is not to sail with any satyrs."

"The satyrs must go!" Hermes stood obstinately on the threshold.

"Hermes," cried Zeus in exasperation. "If you had received as many dispatches as I have from Artemis, the goddess of the forest, describing the torn condition of the forest floor after their parties, you wouldn't send them anywhere. You would try to keep them hidden in the thickets. Their sharp little hooves soar with such spring and land with such assurance that the moss rug of the woodland is permanently damaged in their dancing groves. Yes, permanently! Artemis rages, but

The Spirit of Spring

they wink behind her back and never dance in the same clearing twice. Would you wish such disreputable spirits to go with my son to the east? It wouldn't be seemly."

"But, Zeus, the satyrs are the spirits of all the things Dionysos will leave behind—the woodlands, the vines and the moist dirt. Their leathery ears will remind him of the goats on the hillsides. Their hooves will bring back the racing, the dancing, the meandering, the scampering—all the things one's feet do on a ripe spring meadow. Their horns will remind him of the hard bark of the trees, of the spring around Nysa when the young animals scrape the fuzz off their first horns."

"Nevertheless," Zeus objected, "you are still packing the forest and its livestock, boisterous and seething as it always is, into one small moon-boat! Will this vessel of yours keep afloat? I can't believe such an assortment of creatures is what my boy needs on his first journey. I think food and clothes . . ."

"Can't dance for him, Zeus, or cheer him when he's homesick."

"Are you going to ask me to send his nurses next?"

"Not to Egypt! They're lame!" Hermes exclaimed, then reconsidered. "But I could alert the nymphs. He'll need a female following—like his nurses—and the nymphs would be very excited over the prospect of traveling with Dionysos. Some of them have already left their streams and pools for him. They've learned to manage their flowing chitons and they have a new name. They're called maenads—dancing maidens. Laughter, Dance, Summer Bloom, Bright-Eyes, Revel, Golden Hair, Large Eyes, Flat Nose, Seedpod and

Exile to the East

54   Beauteous—I'm sure they'll be there at the shore this evening."

"What?" cried Zeus.

"Ivy, Peace, Calm and Chaos will be leading them. Now, if I can catch Thyrbas as he dashes off to some woodland party. . . ."

"Not Joyous Disturbance!" Zeus gasped.

"Of course! Who else could lead the satyrs away from their cool forest homes in Greece to sticky Egypt?" Zeus fell back on his embroidered cushions.

"Dionysos is traveling rather heavily, don't you think, Hermes?"

"Not at all, Zeus. Hera is glistening with vengeance. I think a tribe of five hundred disheveled forest sprites would upset the most careful planning."

"You are right, Hermes. Let them all sail to Egypt. . . ."

"Tonight!" finished Hermes and he vanished from the bronze threshold.

Along the shore that night were many fires and a beautiful moon-boat lay cushioned in the arms of a small bay. A grapevine was laced around her mast, and pots of ivy were being stowed beneath her deck. Satyrs, maenads and sileni were crowding toward her bearing small bundles. They were greeting nereids, the nymphs of the deep, and tasting salt water in fascination, some having never been out of their forests before. Many were playing music, others were dancing, and their forms whirled in the firelight like the shadows of tree limbs on a windy day.

Dionysos greeted them from the prow of his ship. He wore a wreath of ivy and grapes, a long purple chiton with embroidered edges, a fawnskin cloak ga-

The Spirit of Spring

thered up at one shoulder with a sparkling gem and
sandals with golden lachets. In his hand he held a
thyrsus trimmed with billowing streamers of grapevines
and ivy. The youth watched the other passengers with
secret wonder, for he had never known when he was
little that every stream, every tree, every mountain
was filled with such whimsical creatures.

Lieutenants Pan and Silenos huddled beside him,
keeping up a steady murmur.

"I don't want to go," said Pan.

"I never could stand the sea," Silenos replied.

"But you're a water sprite."

"I'm a fresh-water sprite."

"Come now, you two!" cried Dionysos. When his
comrades continued to whisper, he burst out impatiently, "Hermes brought me extraordinary tidings today. Did you know that my father is the king of the
gods?"

"Zeus?" breathed Pan and Silenos in unison.

"Zeus himself! We can't stay on the outskirts of
Nysa because Hera hasn't recovered from the rage she
felt at my birth and is pursuing us. . . ."

"Shouldn't Zeus—since he's your father—take you
up to Mount Olympus?" interrupted Silenos.

"Of course not!"

"Why?"

"Because I haven't done anything yet! The Seasons
didn't open the gates of Mount Olympus for Zeus until
he had killed a score of giants, or for Apollo until he
had slain a dragon. . . ."

"Oh, no," gasped Pan. "Is that why we're going to
the east?"

"Pan," Dionysos reasoned. "It's not as though you

Exile to the East

were traveling with a mortal. While my father gave the rose to Aphrodite, the olive to Athena, the corn to Demeter, and the laurel to Apollo, he saved the grapevine for me. Think of that!"

"But what of Hera?"

"Hera!" Dionysos reproved him. "Without Hera we wouldn't see the east! Pan, don't you wonder about the vines of the world, if they're as tangled as the ones we practiced on around Nysa?"

"I wonder if they grow in deserts." Pan's face fell.

"As for the deserts, the withered lands and the parched places," cried Dionysos to Silenos, "we will subdue them immediately with our creepers."

When he thought about his future, it was all Dionysos could do to keep from joining the joyful dance of the forest sprites surging toward the ship.

"What a challenge it will be to make the east fruitful!"

"I wish I were in Arcadia," Pan muttered.

The ship sailed at dawn. Dionysos steered the little boat, and she followed his directions with ease, for many days bobbing daintily along the watery paths of the sea. To watch over her at night, the moon kept always above her and traced her course in the heavens. The maenads, satyrs and sileni enjoyed the moonlight immensely. They consumed large meals of fish and caught huge turtles whose shells they fashioned into lyres. On them they played new music—sea music. Only Pan and Silenos lay below, stricken with helpless agony and homesickness.

As soon as the ship arrived in Egypt, Dionysos was immediately absorbed in his new duties, which included demonstrating everything from the planting of the grapevine to the final harvesting of its fruit. The Egyptian court readily accepted the youth with hair so black that it rivaled their own. They were intrigued with the vines he brought them and curious as to the uses of grapes.

Hera looked down in horror and wondered how she could undo the worthy effects of Dionysos' visit. Then she glimpsed Pan and her face brightened; she went back to her chamber, believing the job would be done for her.

When the Arcadian deity saw the burning tracts of Egypt, he was so dismayed that he left his charges—the satyrs, maenads and sileni—to do all the unpacking and moving. He picked up his pipes and ran. All the way to an Egyptian marketplace he ran, and there he played to the first herd of furry animals he could find, which happened to be camels.

The desert creatures were enchanted. When Pan left, they left too, and ambled away over the dunes in search of the cool, green places and the soft, running water they had known when small and unharnessed.

Pan was captured shortly by the camel-drivers and brought before the Pharaoh, the ruler of Egypt, to be sentenced.

"Pan, what have you done?" cried Dionysos, who was summoned to the Pharaoh's throne room immediately to handle the extraordinary affair.

"Really, Pan," puffed Silenos, who had accompanied the god.

"You should have been planting vines!" reprimanded Dionysos.

"I was playing my pipes," said Pan with dignity.

Exile to the East

"But we're bringing greenery to Egypt!"

"*You're* bringing greenery!" said Pan who regarded every sprout in the desert with loathing. He could never hope to make things grow in a desert.

"Oh, Pan," cried Dionysos in exasperation.

Dionysos turned to the Pharaoh of Egypt, who sat stiffly at the other end of the hall on a great throne.

"This is for you!" he said.

The youth was just able to save his comrade from further harm by giving the Pharaoh a mixing bowl filled with wine, a drink so novel and delicious to the Egyptians that they believed it had been stolen from the table of one of the gods. The court grouped around it eagerly and, as Dionysos ladled the liquid into wine-cups, any thought of Pan slipped from their minds.

"Go practice in the desert!" Silenos said to Pan, as he undid his bonds. "You are making trouble for Dionysos."

"Dionysos! Dionysos! Dionysos!" exclaimed Pan, kicking away the bonds. "Can't anybody in this country speak of anything else?"

"But he's studded the deserts and wastes with orchards and vineyards. Our playmate, Pan, is a god!"

"So am I!" snapped Pan. "A much older one, too, though I live in Arcadia!"

With an angry look at the festivities taking place around the throne, he clattered out and didn't stop until he had reached the Nile. There he turned to his pipes for solace.

The crocodiles had never heard anything like his song. They humped their heavy bodies and jerked them onto the banks. Pan was so lost in his playing that he

The Spirit of Spring

did not see the layers and layers of white teeth that gleamed in the dark mud around him. When he ceased playing and rose to go, the crocodiles were so embittered that they tried to pull him down to their swamp. If it had not been for a band of wandering pygmies who heard his shouts and rescued him, Pan might never have escaped and would have remained in Egypt forever piping a mournful tune in the Nile. Immediately after this, the Arcadian deity took Silenos' advice and set out across the desert.

"Dionysos! Dionysos! Pan is about to be slain!" Silenos shouted at the top of his husky voice. He rushed into a vineyard where Dionysos was pruning a grapevine, surrounded by a host of fascinated Egyptians. "He's been taken prisoner by the temple priests. They insist he has been stealing their sacred cats! Pan, our simple Pan! Whatever are we to do?"

Though Pan had chosen a remote spot in the desert, his notes had flown across the still sands so sweetly that they had been heard by the cats in the temple. The sacred creatures had slunk away to join him. They had curled up on the sand. They had closed their green eyes and had listened, cocking their ears, and every once in a while had twitched all over in enjoyment.

"We'll have to save him!" cried Dionysos.

The tall god strode at once to the temple. Innumerable priests were standing guard over Pan, who could hardly be seen in their midst. Dionysos was granted permission to speak with the prisoner.

"Pan!" Dionysos exclaimed.

Exile to the East

60   He looked at his comrade. Pan's tail had become tangled, his horns unshined, and his cloven hooves dusty and scratched from the sand. He was nothing like the god who had so spiritedly charged the flocks on the hillsides around Nysa.

"Pan! Are you all right? Tell us what happened! You can defend yourself!"

Pan opened his mouth and desperately tried to speak, but no words would come. Dionysos swung around to the priests. They were adament. The horned creature must be destroyed. No sprout, no seed, no creeper would pacify them. Pan clutched his pipes in terror as he listened. He looked to Dionysos, mutely, and his eyes filled with tears.

Dionysos suddenly had an idea.

"Play, Pan!" he cried.

Pan played. The priests forgot what they were saying. In embarrassment they sat down. The notes of the woodland baffled them and seemed to soften the hard lines of their temple and blur the sharp edges of their law. The scribes stretched out their cramped legs and lay down in the corners. The priests shut their eyes, and their heads slouched onto their shoulders. Gradually the temple fell silent and began to dream. Still playing, Pan tiptoed after Dionysos through the vast open gate.

"Dionysos," Pan sobbed with relief. "How did you ever think of that?"

"Pan," said Dionysos gently. "If the Egyptians could be won over by groves and vineyards, they could also be won over by woodland music."

"It does follow," agreed Pan readily. At the thought

The Spirit of Spring

the sprite looked happier than he had been since his arrival in Egypt.

"Furthermore, nothing I planted would ever be complete without your playing," said Dionysos. "All our groves have been so melancholy in Egypt."

"Really, Dionysos?"

"Really," Dionysos assured him. "And now, should you be willing to continue traveling with us . . ."

"I am!" interrupted the older god eagerly.

". . . then we should all go on to India!"

In Egyptian dwellings, maenads were busy explaining new ways of planting and the latest method of training curly vines up the arbors and summerhouses. In the marketplaces, the satyrs were setting a new pace and their sharp hooves smartly tapped the stone walks. They were giving dancing lessons to young Egyptian boys and girls. The sileni stood around accompanying them with tambourines and kettledrums.

At Dionysos' call, the whole town fell still. Then the streets filled with scurrying woodland spirits. Down alleys they pattered, like the fresh spring rain. Down garden paths they swept in gathering torrents until at last they reached their leader's mansion and stood below, awkwardly attentive, their bodies held rigid in the novel stance of quiet.

"We are proceeding to India!" Dionysos announced.

There was a shout of approval, and the maenads began to dance. The satyrs grabbed them by their waists and once more the fat sileni took up their instruments and beat their noisy rhythms. In a band, the

Exile to the East

maenads, satyrs and sileni streamed from the palace and flew off to the vines and flowers they had planted to take clippings to carry to the next land.

Hera fumed in her chamber on Mount Olympus. She had dispatched Dionysos to Egypt because the land had never nurtured any vines. Her ichor—the royal blood of the gods—boiled when she later looked at that particular part of the world. Vines and ivy were sprouting everywhere—even on the Pharaoh's summerhouses—and the Egyptians were worshiping the youth under a different name. And now, that flighty assortment of forest creatures considered themselves members of an important band and were proceeding with all the intensity and assurance of a mighty host toward India. No other god had ever spread his worship so far from Greece.

    Without pausing to consider that she had sent him, Hera shrieked, "He must be stopped!"

Dionysos jogged away from Egypt on the back of a long-legged camel and his followers scampered after him through the deep forests and golden deserts of Arabia, swinging their vines, winecups, thyrsi and tambourines.

    Early one bright morning, a maenad called out shrilly, "Dionysos! Our travels are over! Look!"

    Someone had snapped the bridge over the Euphrates!

    "Branches, stems and baby goats!" swore Silenos in fury, looking at the raging torrent from his sedan chair drawn by four sileni who had almost tumbled into the water out of sheer exhaustion. "We'll never reach India. . . ."

The Spirit of Spring

"Oh, Dionysos!" bleated Pan, "just when I was beginning to catch the flavor of the east!"

"Don't worry, Pan!" Dionysos laughed out loud, hardly able to restrain his excitement. "Remember your misery on the moon-boat. Remember how you said, 'And what will you do about Hera!' Now watch! This is what I'll do about Hera!"

Dionysos ran down to the river and planted a sprig of ivy where the bridge had once been.

Then he shouted to it, "Enoi!"

Miraculously, the sprig threw itself across the shooting stream of water, unraveling, growing larger, stretching forward, spreading outward, straining onward, until finally a bridge of green ivy spanned the circling currents and joined the banks in a leafy arch.

"Dionysos!" Pan was fascinated. "You are a powerful god!"

The bridge was beautiful, far more beautiful than the one Hera had severed. The maenads breezed onto it, enraptured. The little sprig had done its job well and had woven red apples, green vines, white flowers, green ivy, purple berries and green leaves into a brightly colored ribbon. It was wide enough and strong enough for the whole band. It was soft on their bare feet and refreshing to their eyes. Now the water below tinkled airs for them to dance by, and dance they did. They were so pleased with their mid-river grove that it was many hours before Dionysos could persuade them to stop their frolic and cross to the other side—which was, as Dionysos reminded them, the original purpose of the bridge.

"Hey-ho!" cried Thyrbas, the satyr. "There should

be more of these bridges. We could string them from mountain to mountain in Greece. Then we'd never have to climb up, climb down, then up again to reach our higher groves. Just skim one billowing ribbon and no more steep, rocky paths. Give us more energy for dancing. What do you say, Bright-Eyes?"

"Artemis won't love you, but I will," rippled the maenad. "Here's a quince for you, Thyrbas."

She threw the love apple to the satyr, who caught it easily.

"Here's Persia for me," shrieked Pan and flew off the bridge.

He landed on the other side, with both hooves planted firmly in the sand. He flung back his head, took such a breath that his chest almost burst, and loosed a yell. The whole country heard it and fell speechless. Awestruck, it awaited the vast horde of exhilarated creatures who would sail down its narrow roads and turn them into highways, who would tear through its few woodlands and leave them dancing groves.

Dionysos' band streaked through Persia at an astonishing pace and pressed on past the Bactrian strongholds. When they reached the border of India, there was a shriek of laughter from Mount Olympus.

"He'll soon wish he had fallen into the Euphrates!" cried Hera gleefully from her watchpost. "How will he fare in India, where savage animals roam and the land is more barren than the deserts of Egypt! Now, even Zeus will forget about him!"

"Incredible!" exclaimed Zeus. "Do you see that line of green moving like an arrow into the heart of India? That's my son planting the grapevine!"

The Spirit of Spring

"How extraordinary, Zeus," declared Hermes.

"Oh, that grapevine," cried Zeus with delight. "It's better than the rose, the daffodil, the anemone, the lily or the iris."

"It's beautiful," agreed Hermes.

"Beautiful?" echoed Zeus. "Useful, Hermes! It gives both food and drink to mortals."

"Here, Zeus," said Hermes soothingly. "You must have some more nectar."

"Just to see those upraised winecups in India makes me thirsty," Zeus said excitedly, holding out his goblet.

They both quieted as Hera floated in, looking magnificent. The queen of the gods had just swathed herself in her favorite raiment to watch the downfall of Dionysos. She had arranged her hair in shining curls and when she walked up to them she brought with her the beautiful fragrance of scented oil.

"Oh," she said, feigning surprise at discovering Zeus upon his throne. "I can see by the turn of your head that you're looking at India—some starved travelers, no doubt . . ."

There was a startled silence.

". . . pursued by wild beasts."

She smiled and sat down. She glanced out the window, then clutched the sides of her throne in fury. India had turned as green as the outskirts of Nysa and Dionysos was astride a tiger.

"The Indian king will not be hospitable!" she spat out ominously.

Dionysos' staunch band of followers, who had been brought up in the most luxuriant forests on earth, had never seen anything like the land that was opening up around Dionysos.

India was so green—meadow green, tree green, bush green, moss green, vine green, sprout green, all the green they could wish for and more than they could stand. Mountains, groves, pools, lakes, forests waited for their stillness to be shattered, waited as presents tied up with knotted vines ready to be unwrapped. The color was too rich, the scent too sweet for the satyrs, maenads and sileni to keep their balance.

They rolled over the countryside, reeling from exuberance. Animals trod beside them, silently, stealthily, feeling for the strange power behind this man who led them. Man? God? The flat-footed elephants fell in a heap, imitating his dancing. But they picked themselves up and followed him anyway. Tigers, leopards, lions and panthers streaked through the underbrush beside his path. Antelopes challenged him to races.

Everywhere that Dionysos led the sprites there was something to do, something to eat, something to drink, something to look at, something to hear. With cinnamon, clove and tamarind they spiced their food. They munched breadfruit and drained the milk from coconuts. Upon the brow of mountains they posed themselves just long enough to fill their chests with the breath of sandalwood. Then down they careened, and plunging into dark water, they would bathe with the shy lotus blossoms in hidden mountain pools. Each night all would have to drag themselves back to camp, only to fall unconscious on their blankets, wreathed from horn to hoof, or head to toe, with madhari flowers.

"Dionysos, this is your work, isn't it?" Pan whis-

The Spirit of Spring

pered confidentially one morning. "You did bring this abundance to India, didn't you? There are as many grapes here, and as much corn and barley as there was sand in the desert. The whole countryside is wet. In fact, everywhere you lead us becomes wet with wine, honey, oil, milk and water. The villages are splashing in it!"

Pan sauntered away blithely without bothering about an answer. Dionysos, however, looked thoughtful. He had watched small shoots sprout into blossom as breathlessly as his followers, and Pan was correct. He had brought overwhelming abundance to India, more greenness than he ever dreamed he could produce when he first set out from the gardens of Nysa.

The moment Dionysos' band felt his thoughtfulness, they sprang to his side as if to drive it away, beating their drums and slapping tambourines. Dionysos turned to them. His eyes began to sparkle. The sunlight caught him and outlined him, skimming over the gold-embroidered edges of his long mantle. Maenads seized his arms, filled his winecup and led him away to laughter and song, to honey and sweet wine.

"How wonderful to be a god," he thought suddenly, "and to have vines and creepers and flowers to adorn the earth one loves and to sustain it. When I am through, there will be nowhere I haven't brought them!"

While dancing feet were tapping the earth with joyous unconcern, messengers were racing each other back to the palace of the Indian king to be the first with the news. As they hurtled in one after another, and as

Exile to the East

their tales of Dionysos and his band grew more numerous and more fantastic, the whole palace gradually filled with shouts of unsuppressed laughter.

Pan did not know what the messengers were saying about him, and it would not have mattered if he had, for he never bothered himself with what other people thought.

"Dionysos!" he called the god's name in a loud whisper. "I think I've found an Indian water nymph."

He had been intent on a particularly lively stream all morning, and now that afternoon was coming on, he had convinced himself that there really was a delicate, brown-eyed creature in it, staring up at him adoringly. He was piping gently.

"Dionysos!" Silenos came wheezing up from the other direction. "Something awful has happened. I struck that boulder with my thyrsus and look what came out."

"I see nothing unusual," said the god soothingly. "There's a white stream of milk flowing from the rock. You haven't lost your talent."

"You just taste that trickle of . . . of . . ." Silenos said bitterly.

Pan had lost interest in his stream (actually the nymph had not moved at all in the past hour and he did not feel like admitting there might not be one). He raced Dionysos to the boulder, arrived first and thrust his face into the foaming white liquid, lapping furiously with his red tongue. When he was surfeited, he shook himself and sputtered, "That madcap goat! It's buttermilk!"

"Silenos," Dionysos laughed. "You are turning into an Indian."

The Spirit of Spring

"But I don't like buttermilk," Silenos replied peevishly.

On the one hand he was flattered by Dionysos' remark, and on the other hand he was incensed by Pan's laughter and the vile, sour, heavy, unpleasant liquid pouring out of the rock. Watching it splash and burble was finally too much for him and he could contain himself no longer. A wave of homesickness seized him.

"I don't like it, Dionysos. When can we go home to Greece? I can't stand it!"

"All the more for me!" Pan liked anything that was abundant, and he gurgled happily as he lapped.

"Now behave yourselves, you two!" Dionysos' mood changed swiftly these days. Sternly he said to his creatures, "We must continue through the villages and approach the city. If the king receives us, I will turn all his rivers into wine and crown the peaks of his mountains with grapevines and ivy. If he does not receive us, he must be conquered. We must then prepare to fight our first battle and to establish a reign of planting, nurturing and harvesting. No more sport today, Pan! Maenads! Gather up your vines! Satyrs! Sort the grapes! Pan! Feed the animals! Silenos! Silenos, what had you better do? Bright-Eyes, bring him an amphora of milk!"

As soon as the chores were finished, Dionysos gave the cry, "Enoi!" and the band plunged on.

"He is a madman," proclaimed the philosopher to the Indian court. "This collection of horns, drums, flying robes and ivy-twined staffs is unique in our history. The leader is a ridiculous figure. On his head is a

Exile to the East

wreath of grapes. He wears a long purple robe and golden sandals. As for his two lieutenants—one is a short, fat man dressed in yellow, who wobbles along with a staff. The other . . ."

"Please let me tell about the other!" the second philosopher cried.

Upon learning the details of Pan, the Indian court burst out laughing.

Suddenly there was a clatter in the corridor and a messenger rushed into the throne room. "My lord, they have arrived!"

"We'll send out our chambermaids," said the king. The nobles tittered.

"After all," continued the king, "why should we deploy our brilliant troops, our sharp lancers, our nimble elephants against a wreathed leader, a piper, a goat soldier and a chorus of crazy female dancers?"

"But they're at the gates of the city!" cried the messenger.

"Hooray!" Silenos could be heard shouting in the distance. "Our Dionysos is the son of Zeus!"

The Indian nobles were livid.

"Tonight those maenads will be tying our daughters' hair ribbons!" one cried.

"The satyrs will be herding our elephants!"

"The sileni will be serving our banquets!"

The whole court took up arms. They saddled and bridled their elephants. They put huge towers on their backs, and forth they sallied in one long line.

Dionysos' tactics were simpler. He marshaled his troops from a chariot drawn by panthers. Instead of squeezing the sprites into close formation, he stationed Pan to cover the right wing and Silenos to cover the left. Behind Pan marched the satyrs, and behind Silenos the sileni.

Dionysos let loose his rallying cry, "Enoi!"

In the rear the maenads struck their tambourines. The cymbals clanged. A satyr held up his trumpet to make the charge official. The jackasses hee-hawed.

The satyrs stormed forward and slashed at the feet of the elephants with little spears concealed beneath their thyrsi. The maenads dived in after them, darting their pet serpents in the faces of the Indian host, letting the snakes sizzle and sting their opponents. The bedlam, the color, the assortment of jackasses, horns, tails, tambourines, panthers, flying chitons, serpents, elephants and leopards overpowered the Indian king and his army. They had no counterattack for this extraordinary line of battle, which did not seem to advance as in war, but circled as in a dance. And who was responsible for those periodic yells? The Indians were so confused they hardly knew which way to retreat. The king was last seen hurtling over the eastern horizon, clinging to the neck of a runaway elephant.

India fell. Hera was wild with wrath. How could the trained forces of the Indians have surrendered to Dionysos' haphazard band? But Zeus smiled as he watched Dionysos establish a new rule that gave the nobles' and philosophers' former positions to outstanding satyrs and well-informed sileni. Calling his maenads together, Dionysos even formed an office of dance. Its members spread through every corner of the kingdom, teaching the natives to clap a tambourine

Exile to the East

and frolic. India prospered during Dionysos' reign. Wine, oil, milk, water and honey seemed to burst from every rock, boulder and pebble of the land.

"Silenos," Dionysos called one morning to his comrade, who was sitting alone on a boulder dreaming of Greece with his round eyes open. "Silenos! I think you can gather your belongings."

"I have them with me perpetually," said the sprite as he pointed listlessly to his tiny bundle and added, longingly, "in case we leave India in a hurry." He suddenly woke up. "What did you say, Dionysos? Packing? Is that what you mean? Oh! Can we go immediately?"

"We could," Dionysos hesitated as he said this and smiled, "except for the others. We'll have to wait a few moments for them. But we're going any time. Our work is done!"

"What? We're leaving?" Pan bounded up excitedly. He had seen all he wished of the east. Now, every night, dreams of Arcadia recurred with great vividness, and he longed for his home meadows.

"Yes, but first I am going to design a grove," Dionysos announced.

"Always delay . . . always delay," moaned Silenos.

"A beautiful grove on the banks of the Indus River," Dionysos enlarged upon his plan.

"In honor of me?" Silenos asked at once.

"No, silly, *me*," Pan retorted.

"In honor of both of you," Dionysos intervened. "There will be three springs of cold water. One is in honor of the satyrs, one is in honor of Pan and the last is in honor of Silenos. Once a year, every mortal who

The Spirit of Spring

is able must drink from his proper spring. Little boys will drink from the satyrs' pool, and they will grow up healthy and strong. Grown men will drink from Pan's pool, and they will be successful in love. . . ."

Pan looked at Dionysos dubiously, remembering the episode of the Indian water nymph. Then the sprite gave a slight shrug.

"Of course, every maenad in the band is in love with me," he murmured.

"And my pool?" pressed Silenos.

"Elderly men will drink from it and become eloquent."

"Oh," sighed Silenos ecstatically. "Will they really?"

"Of course," said Dionysos. "Their voices will be as resonant as they were hoarse before. No one will be able to stem the interchange of words. And if an old man who has drunk from your spring is prevented by the setting of the sun from finishing his tale, then join him there the next year when he drinks. Listen closely and you shall hear . . ."

"What?" breathed Silenos, so thrilled he could hardly speak.

"The ending of the story from the year before!" Dionysos grinned boyishly and grabbed Pan's arm. The two frisked off to pack their fawnskins, leaving Silenos alone and enchanted upon his rock.

At dawn the next day, Dionysos, Pan, Silenos and the woodland sprites set out. They left India and marched away through Asia, carrying brightly colored birds and cinnamon trees as souvenirs and leading a

Exile to the East

herd of assorted eastern animals, from spotted leopards to elephants.

They made their way in irregular, buoyant fashion across Medea, over the deserts where they roofed each oasis with evergreen creepers and straight through the cities where the streets were paved with glittering mosaics. Occasionally they left behind a maenad to give the Asians dancing lessons or a fountain that poured only wine.

"I can't believe it. Soon I will be in Greece," chortled Pan.

"To see grapevines growing wild again," sighed Dionysos.

The caravan rolled on—panthers, maenads, tigers, satyrs and sileni. As they trekked through Phrygia, the road became hotter and hotter and hotter, but now the sprites were too intent on Greece to pause—even to plant a vine.

"Pan, play your pipes," Dionysos commanded wearily. "The elephants are going to sleep."

Pan pulled out his pipes and began to play, but he was so exhausted that his notes came out a lullaby. Hearing them, the whole troop wanted to lie down and sleep. The voices of the sileni were silent; their throats were too parched for them to shout and sing. The maenads' feet were blistered; never had they trod such an uncomfortable road. The band was tottering along when suddenly Dionysos said to Pan, "Where's Silenos?"

The question was passed all the way back to the last elephant before it received an answer—no one had seen Silenos.

The Spirit of Spring

"I knew we wouldn't reach home without disaster," 75
said Pan.

"Now, Pan," Dionysos replied. "He can't have
gone far."

Silenos was unaware of the concern he was caus-
ing the caravan. He had wandered off from the company in an effort to locate a boulder from which he
could obtain a quick drink. In the process he had
stumbled into the most beautiful garden he had ever
beheld. It was a rose garden, and the roses it nurtured
were sixty-petaled and bloomed a red that rivaled the
setting sun.

"What beautiful roses," mused Silenos. In awe
the sprite tiptoed down the path of seashells and
acanthus leaves. "It is much the best place I have
ever seen."

With these words he forgot Dionysos, he forgot
the caravan. He just tumbled into a stream in his
eagerness to quench his thirst. He emerged only when
he felt thoroughly water-logged, and taking one last
draught of sweet water, he sank down to sleep—forever,
he hoped.

"Where can he be?" Pan was asking Dionysos days
later. "I have asked every nymph in every scrawny tree
for miles about and not a one has seen him."

"I think I know why," said Dionysos. "I was just
talking with the nymph from the fountain of Inna and
he's been with her."

"Ah, I knew it! He has chosen her over us, the
old goat!" Pan could not help laughing now that he
knew his comrade was safe.

"He drank from her springs," said Dionysos, "and

Exile to the East

DENVER
PUBLIC LIBRARY
NOV 1971
CITY & COUNTY OF DENVER

slept for hours afterward. Then Midas' gardeners captured him—Midas is the king who owns the rose garden. His greed is without parallel. Midas had a suspicion he was ours, but kept him anyway for entertainment at a feast. He thought he wouldn't have to pay. You know as well as I do, Pan, what Silenos does to his listeners in the guise of entertaining them. He made fools out of them all with his preposterous tales. The nobles believed every word until at the end Silenos stated that nothing he had said ever happened. You can imagine their wrath. The guests have declared revenge on King Midas for giving such a bad banquet, and Silenos is locked in the gardener's shed with a heap of pointed trowels for a bed. . . . There, King Midas' messengers are coming now."

"My lord," said one of the messengers. "Your servant came to our king in a state of horrible thirst and raving delirium. Despite his frequent outbursts, which have ruined the feasts in our quiet kingdom, our king has shown him the utmost kindness and hospitality."

"I am glad," Dionysos said. His eyes glittered brightly.

"Will you please come to fetch him."

"With pleasure."

Dionysos and Pan followed the messengers to the palace of the Phrygian king. Midas came to greet them, so eager to make a regal entrance that he tripped over his robe.

"King Midas," Dionysos hailed him and helped him to his feet. "Your messenger has already told me how much I have inconvenienced you and your princely

"Yes," said King Midas, and he looked at Dionysos,
wondering how powerful the young god was. He had
heard some fabulous tales, and he replied, "I would
like everything I touch to turn to gold."

Pan let out a shrill whistle.

"If that is all you wish, then I am happy to grant
it," said Dionysos.

"At last, Dionysos has made a mistake," thought
Pan, "a mistake I can tease him about for the rest of
the journey." Dionysos only smiled genially.

Having been granted his favor, the king had nothing
more to say to either Dionysos or Pan. They were given
a most belligerent Silenos and were shown to the portal.
With Silenos huffing and puffing loudly over the stu-
pidity of granting Midas' wish, the three trooped back
to the caravan.

Not too much later, King Midas' messenger arrived
again.

"Dionysos," he addressed Dionysos in a new
fashion. He could barely speak, and when he did, he
spoke humbly. "King Midas has turned the kingdom
to gold—the musicians, the gardens, the gardeners, his
neighbors, the food and the wine. He is stretched out
on a golden brick that was once his couch. He is sleep-
less, hungry, thirsty, lonely, bored, blinded and unhappy. Can you do something at once. He was not a
bad king, only. . . ."

"No!" said Silenos abruptly.

"One moment, Silenos," Dionysos silenced his
comrade. He turned to the messenger. "Tell that poor,

foolish king of yours to travel to the mouth of the stream Patroclus. There he is to bathe and scrub the golden touch from his body."

"Why that particular stream, Dionysos?" Silenos asked after the messenger had left.

"The gold that will come off will flow down the river and later fill the treasuries of a king whose name will be Croesus."

"I'd like to be as rich as Croesus!" exclaimed Silenos.

Pan was busily making calculations in the dirt with a hoof as to how much gold there would be, taking into account Midas' wide girth.

"Couldn't we wait until Midas had bathed and take the gold back with us?"

"Of course not!" cried Dionysos. "We have things greater than gold awaiting us. Enoi! Pan! Silenos! Bright-Eyes! Thyrbas! Summer Bloom! Revel! On to Greece!"

The Spirit of Spring

CHAPTER FIVE
Return to Greece

*Jubilantly the maenads, satyrs and sileni left
Asia and swept under a rainbow into Greece.*

82   *J*UBILANTLY THE MAENADS, SATYRS AND SILENI LEFT ASIA and swept under a rainbow into Greece. Dionysos looked over the countryside in rapture, taking up his ivy and vines as if to garland the waiting earth immediately. At last he was in his homeland. This thought would have caused him to whirl furiously on the spot had he had anyone by his side who felt his particular joy. As it was, the members of his band were bounding, leaping and scurrying off in different directions to a bubbling stream, a flower-strewn meadow or a still grove which they were sure would be nearby to welcome them back and remind them of the green nooks they had left long ago. Dionysos could hear them breathlessly sharing the news of his arrival with the sprites who had stayed behind. He stood there, listening and looking at all his creatures. Although he was their leader, he himself did not know what was within the great forests or over the high hills or even beyond the clear shores they knew so well.

"Pan, are you there?" called Silenos shrilly from the back of his jackass. He had just put his head down a hole that contained a wasp's nest instead of honey.

Pan didn't want to ride. He wanted to feel the Greek soil, and he was romping ecstatically in circles around the milling throng.

"Of course I'm here," he cried as his circle took him past Silenos again.

"Pan!" cried Silenos, managing to escape the cloud of wasps. "In one hour, see if you can gather more olives, grapes and figs than I can eat. Go!"

"Shame, Silenos!" Dionysos cried, coming out of his reverie. "Taking advantage of Pan's high spirits! I think he's collected the whole Greek countryside and put it into wreaths. Fruits, ivy, flowers and vines—my band looks like a wandering market."

"It doesn't matter, Dionysos," cried Pan from a meadow. "I'll gather anything Silenos wants, now that I'm home—or at least halfway to Arcadia."

As Dionysos' remarkable column advanced into Greece, its path grew darker. The rainbow faded and storm clouds thickened into a high dome overhead.

From above, Hera could easily distinguish the bright colors of the caravan. Red, yellow, blue, pink and orange were not easily lost on a matt-green countryside; nor was a myriad of panthers, tigers, lions and elephants ideal for secret travel. The women streaming from their villages to dance with Dionysos were soon observed, as well as the dryads stepping down from their trees.

Hera had prepared her plan. It was not difficult. There were kings and townfolk who would not tolerate this figure who had conquered the east and now swept down through the mountains and villages of Greece, gathering followers as he came. They had never before heard of such behavior in a god. The gods they knew and worshiped stayed on Mount Olympus and did not wander over the earth, and if they did, they went alone, not escorted by hundreds of dancing followers, some of whom had tails. The young, black-haired son of a mortal princess had no regular worship. He just traveled along, planting ivy and grapevines, teaching everyone to make wine and then drinking it with them, holding festivals and dancing for hours with unrestrained delight.

In truth, Dionysos was a new being and brought a new joy—the joy of being on earth and not Mount Olympus. This joy only a great god could give, but to those who did not like the earth, he was a dangerous figure. His unmasked pleasure in plants, flowers and animals was an insult against the true gods, who knew the earth was an extremely disagreeable place— which held the terrors of poverty and old age—and stayed far away on Mount Olympus.

As tales of this new god and his devoted followers became more frequent, some people rebelled. Their antagonism was such that they no longer thought he was a god. They scorned what he said. How could men be happy with only an amphora of wine, a vine spray or a basket of wild figs. Soon all men, incited by this extraordinary person, would consider themselves kings. Never! Hera was not alone in her hatred of Dionysos. It was growing greater all the while.

There was a certain king at this time ruling over Thrace. His name was Lycurgus. With malice, he began to eye the joy, the well-being and the prosperity of the troop marching through his kingdom. He was envious of their sport. He hated the sound of the tympanums, clappers, flutes and tambourines that rang out over the countryside, and he hated the great silence, the blissfulness, that came after the dancing had finished in his groves. The happiness and well-being of the maenad who rode on a lion, or even a donkey, the careless gaiety of the satyr who watered the vine nettled him until he could stand it no longer.

He took the goad he used on his oxen and ran off in pursuit of the caravan that eased over the plains, idled by the streams and camped in the meadows. He lashed out against the brightness of Dionysos' wagon with his ox-goad. He slashed the sleeping maenads and they fled. It was so unexpected. They had never been treated like that before. The maenads dropped their thyrsi and wreaths on the ground in terror, and tripped over each other in their efforts to reach the nearest tree. Terror-stricken, the other sprites jumped onto clouds, hid under mosses or plunged into streams.

Dionysos was astonished.

"Why is this happening to me in my homeland, Silenos? Why does he hate me?" he cried, but Silenos was not by his side. "Pan! Pan! Where are you?"

Pan was nowhere to be found. The scene by the wagons had turned to bedlam so terrible that not a sprite could be recognized. There was only a shocking confusion of fawnskins, horns, tails, tambourines, wreaths and fleeing figures.

Dionysos dropped his winecup as the mad king sprang toward him, cutting the air with his ox-goad. Dionysos escaped. He leapt over the green expanse of shoreland and into the sea beyond. Thetis, the goddess of the waves, came upon him crouched by her doorstep in the depths. He was alone, trembling violently. She took him into her cavern and comforted him.

Meanwhile, Lycurgus continued his raid. He scattered the donkeys and grabbed at the chitons of fleeing maenads.

Dionysos did not yet realize the immense power which was his through birth, but the earth—the forests, hillsides and meadows—knew and quaked in fear. Suddenly, it seemed, the whole universe grew still.

The small son of Lycurgus had just toddled up to see what his father was doing. He tugged at the king's knees and begged him in childish tones to explain. Lycurgus paused to see what was entangling him. He looked down, but in his wickedness he saw a brown vine.

This he immediately hacked to pieces, screaming, "No! No! You lifeless vegetation, you will not stop me! You will not trap my limbs, nor will one green shoot of yours escape my goad. I will destroy you forever! Take this! Again! There. . . ."

"You must go, now, Dionysos," Thetis said to the god softly, once the sounds of earth had picked up again—the birds and the cicadas. "I hear a king weeping by a devastated grove. He has just killed his son. The maenads are picking up their thyrsi. You must go back."

"W–w–where shall I go on to?" stammered Dionysos, wishing he had never returned to Greece. He was terrified by the fearful role he had played in this unexpected disaster.

"You must go through Greece," murmured the goddess of the waves.

"But H–hera . . ." Dionysos tripped over the queen

of the gods' name, for he had never before spoken it.
Throughout the east, she had seemed far away and
remote. But now that he was in Greece, he began to
feel her nearness.

"She is a strange goddess," said Thetis, "and it is
not only you she persecutes. Once, long ago, when her
son Hephestos was just a baby, she threw him off the
edge of Mount Olympus because he was lame. I nursed
him here in my cavern, revived him and sent him back
and told him to forgive her. You must do the same
someday. But now, Dionysos, travel to every city in
Greece, as you have traveled to every city in the east.
Cultivate the tangled vines and plant new ones. And
do not stop there. Give the mortals fresh flowers and
orchards laden with fruit. You are a great god, although
you do not know it, and you will come naturally—
without any conniving—into the company of gods. However, if mortal kings oppose your advance, you must
punish them, for Hera is stirring their wrath. You must
prove yourself more powerful than she if you wish to
remain in Greece and one day live on Mount Olympus.
Here, I will give you a wreath of celery leaves to wear
for luck. Remember me and remember what I have
said."

Dionysos left. He could still feel that gentle presence at his side as he wandered along the sandy strand,
looking for the path that would lead him back to his
followers.

"She mentioned punishment," he thought. "I shall
imprison Lycurgus in a rocky cave until he learns to
honor the forces of nature. That is fair, I think. He
has killed his son."

Dionysos was sad, however, although he had decreed such a lenient punishment. Punishing Greek kings was not the same as dethroning oriental ones. Must he do it throughout his journey, as Thetis had prophesied? Ah, well! Pan stole up behind him, and a little forest hand crept shyly around the god's shoulders to comfort him.

The days that followed were beautiful and clear. Each morning as Dionysos arose he glimpsed a new color. Some mornings it would be purple and all the purple flowers in Greece would dazzle him, and every other pink, blue, yellow or red flower would seem so pale beside them.

Pan wove hundreds of wreaths as they rollicked along. His hands were raw. Violets, crocuses, hyacinths, tulips, daisies—he bound them together and tripped Silenos and lassoed sleeping maenads with their flowery coils. Then, one day, he missed a nymph and looped a panther, who leapt up. Pan hid. The panther growled, then nosed the wreath and went back to sleep, his strong neck feeling the touch of wildflowers and his mind recognizing the miracle of a land where animals followed gods and were wreathed like kings.

At Orchomenus the priests were jubilant over Dionysos' arrival. The village boomed and clacked with preparations for a feast in his honor. Men designed little false faces that looked like the god's and hung them on the trees and vines for good luck—to make them grow. Women washed their chitons three times over in the village fountain so that theirs might shine the brightest in the harvest procession. They dyed their hair ribbons new colors and wove them into wreaths with bunches of grapes and ivy. They begged their

husbands to purchase for them the choicest fawnskins
in the land, soft red or tawny beige.

Maenads were seen bustling through the streets on important missions, scouting for dancing places or sampling grapes. Incense floated through the village. Sumptuous offerings were heaped everywhere, dedicated to the Deliverer from Sorrow, Son of Thunder, Twiner of Violets, Planter of Vines, and work was the concern of no one, except the daughters of Minyas, the richest man in Greece.

New days dawned, blissful days, when the only thing under the sky worth doing was dancing. In the square, in the courtyard, in the kitchen, to the side of an idle loom, in ships, in pastures, feet were hesitantly feeling for new rhythms. Everywhere this was taking place—except in the home of the daughters of Minyas.

There were three daughters of Minyas. Their names were Leuconoe, Alcithoe and Arsippe, and they lived in the last cottage on the village street. Over the years their prunelike faces had shriveled into perpetual scowls.

They frowned on the preparations for the grand feast. They complained that Dionysos was not the son of Zeus. How could anyone compare that chattering of castanets in the distance with Zeus's magnificent roll of thunder? However, since it was not possible for them to complain more on one day than on the next, no one gave a moment's thought to the three bent women, and last-minute arrangements continued frantically.

While the women hung false faces in the dancing groves and the children planted violets on their floors, Leuconoe, Alcithoe and Arsippe sat weaving. Their work would not be put aside, if they had anything to say, nor would they shirk their tasks like the foolish servant girls over such a flimsy excuse as a new god.

"Why, he's just a man!" Leuconoe said bitterly. She watched the procession marching outside the window and quickly turned back to her work.

"The Indian-Slayer! Bah!" rejoined Alcithoe.

"The imprisonment of Lycurgus! Rumors! All rumors!" Arsippe shouted the last so that it might reach the dancing figures wending their way into a forest ablaze with torches and bonfires.

When the villagers of Orchomenus had vanished into the glowing forest, the one cottage at the end of the street became quite dark in comparison with the shining grove in the distance, quite barren in comparison with the noise of good food and rich meat being served and appreciated, and quite still in comparison with the festive music and sounds of dancing. The hags huddled together. To pass the drab hours, they decided to tell each other stories.

"I do not know whether I should tell the tale of the maiden who was turned into a fish, or the tale of a nymph who turned boys into fish, or the tale of how the stain of blood . . ." began Arsippe.

"I like the one about blood," pressed Alcithoe.

"I rather like that one, too," agreed Leuconoe. "It will probably deal with misfortune."

"Yes," Arsippe replied dreamily. "It is a good tale of misfortune that makes the long evening seem short."

"Then perhaps you should tell the tale of the shepherd who was turned into a stone," said Leuconoe.

"Yes," said Alcithoe, "and why did that happen? Because he wasn't where he should have been. . . ."

"With his sheep," said Leuconoe, adding, "Don't

The Spirit of Spring

his beloved Smilex."

"Those were the days when gods had power and stature," said Arsippe in annoyance, "when brave men and dutiful women did not follow mortals. Now any person who plants a vine can be a god and be worshiped as the son of Zeus!"

Suddenly—crash! There was a thump, a yell and a raucous bellow! The walls jumped. Flutes chirped and little pointed horns butted the tables and chairs into corners. The center of the room was being cleared. Currents of myrrh and saffron flew through the air as daintily as spring zephyrs. There was an explosion of cymbals, kettledrums and tambourines that transformed the silence of the house to bedlam.

The sisters' first thought was for their weaving. They grabbed the material with intent to flee, but as they pulled it off the loom into their arms, they discovered their handiwork was nothing more than a tangle of vines haphazardly plaited, with clusters of grapes hanging from the areas of the design that had once been woven in purple. The remaining threads in the basket were tendrils of vines, small and delicate.

The building felt a tremor and the earth did, too. A black-haired figure had put his foot on the doorstep of the cottage. Oil lamps flared and flickered odd shapes onto the walls. Beasts of all sorts began to whine, to snort, to gurgle and howl. The sisters fought to reach the door first. Their hard nails sliced each other's eyes and ripped each other's cheeks and tore each other's garments. Alcithoe knocked Leuconoe down, stamping over the fallen form in her impatience to find a deserted room in which she could hide. She stumbled into every chamber with her sisters at her heels, but in every one a panther crouched, staring at the entrance with huge, unblinking eyes.

Suddenly there was an overwhelming radiance. It was as though the fire within the hearth had felt constricted and had burst forth to see the other chambers. Dionysos, child of the great light, was inside the cottage. In the unbearable glare, the hags sought darkness. They craved gloom. How they wanted it, but there were no shadows anywhere. Instead, panthers, satyrs, maenads and sileni were dancing joyously in the center of every light-filled room.

In desperation the sisters climbed the ladder to the attic. Its blackness welcomed them, and they paused a moment in relief, only to discover their legs were no longer free. Over their arms, a membrane was spreading and transforming them into velvety wings. As they tried to complain, their voices spiraled up to a series of squeaks. Gradually they felt themselves being lifted, not on soaring feathers but on thin wings so frail that anyone could see through them. Panicked, they flew around in circles bumping into each other, until finally they escaped out the window and into the night.

They never approached the trees, for they hated forests. They never approached the light, for they hated fires. Anything twined or threadlike drove them mad. Straight into human hair they would rush when they saw it, as though to destroy it! Threads enraged their tiny minds and brought back the memory of that frightful night when they still had their human form.

The Spirit of Spring

Dionysos cried to his followers, "I have turned them into bats. They hated the light. They despised singing and dancing. And bats love darkness, squeaky tones, cobwebs and deserted attics. I have named their breed vespertiliones—evening flutterers. How gentle that sounds. It's the least I could do for the three old hags. Upon those dwelling on the dark side of life, it's useless to waste a human form."

Dionysos continued his travels. The maenads, in their laughter over the bats, had recovered from the stings of Lycurgus' goad and were dancing around the moving caravan. When exhausted, they would collapse in oriental splendor on the backs of panthers and fan themselves with plaited leaves. No one ever worried about food. Satyrs struck the ground and apple trees would arise, thick with fruit. Sileni bumped into rocks and milk would shower out all over them.

Dionysos issued invitations to every woodland sprite to join him, and every one responded with joy. His easy command and laughing leadership attracted even the most freedom-loving of the forest beings.

The naiads rose out of their brooks to meet him. The potamiads left their rivers. The oreads jumped down from their mountains to frolic with him, and the nereids swam up from the sea. The animals of the meadows scampered after him and tapped their cloven hooves in double time. As they had once flocked to Pan, they now flocked to him, but although they had left Pan whenever the song from his pipes fell silent, they would never leave Dionysos, for he was song itself.

"Remember," Pan would say with great seriousness

when they came to him to learn how to make their thyrsi, "don't come if you're going to complain."

No one ever did. Who would? Each night they slept on beds of soft grass and each day they feasted on herbs, nuts, berries, wine and fresh milk. Furthermore, every morning they took as long a bath as they wished in a mountain pool.

The women of Tanagra immediately accepted Dionysos as a god upon his arrival in their village for the night. After he left, they practiced his dances over and over again. Finally they were ready to dance before the whole town, not around a statue of the god—for Dionysos would not approve—but around a simple pillar draped with all the wonderful things he had brought them—honeycombs, flowers, fruits, ivy, grapes and vines.

The chorus flocked down to the sea to purify themselves, but before they could do so, a sea monster rose out of the water and attacked them. The women fled back to the temple and prayed to Dionysos, begging him to come to their aid, since they could not dance in his honor without a ritual bath in the sea.

"Silenos," Dionysos said. The caravan had passed from the village. "I hear someone calling. Can you make it out? What about you, Pan?"

"I can only hear a flock of sheep in the next meadow, waiting to be scattered by me," exclaimed Pan, who listened for other sounds than Dionysos.

"I can't hear a thing," Silenos was still a second, "except for the grapes ripening."

"No," said Dionysos quietly. "It's something else.

People who worship me are in trouble. Come, we must help them."

That night, Dionysos, Pan and Silenos went back to the village. They peered here and there among the baskets of grapes, figs and apples. Nothing was amiss. They left the grove and tiptoed down to the shore.

"Look!" cried Pan in a whisper.

There they saw the sea monster. It was a fearsome-looking beast, zigzagging along the rocks with its nose to the ground. The monster was making its way up the shore in the direction of the honey and grapes and wine and figs that had been put aside for the festival in Dionysos' honor.

"How dare he?" exclaimed Silenos.

"How dare *she?*" cried Dionysos, with a sharp look up at the darkened sky.

The three tore forward in their usual fashion. The sea monster angrily reared onto its hind legs as they came. Pan yelled. Silenos bellowed. Dionysos hurled a well-aimed thyrsus, and the sea monster popped like a bubble.

"How extraordinary!" exclaimed Pan, staring at the carcass. "There wasn't anything to it."

"It must have been sent just to disrupt my festival," said Dionysos as they tripped away gaily to rejoin their band, leaving the monster on the beach.

"That's undoubtedly what happened," agreed Silenos, stopping to carry off a large portion of the grapes and apples they had protected from the beast.

Hera, when the news trickled back to Mount Olympus, did not like the speed of Dionysos' victory over the creature she had dispatched to Tanagra any more than she liked the victory itself. Despite the hatred of kings and crones, which she fanned like a fire, he was becoming far too popular in Greece. Swiftly she started a rumor in the small Boeotian village.

"The sea monster did attack the women," began the rumor, "but it was not killed by Dionysos. A crafty man of Tanagra put out a bowl of honey, and the monster, attracted by its fragrance, came at once to devour it and. . . ."

Hera had lit the spark. The next day the countryside was crackling with the news.

One villager said to another in a screeching whisper, "Why, that leathery old thing drank up the honey and flung itself onto the beach to sleep. . . ."

"And then you know what happened . . ." another burst out.

"Dionysos killed him," said a girl who was to dance that evening in his festival.

"Rubbish!" the woman replied, turning upon her. "It was the man from Tanagra who slew him. But would you believe this?" She turned to all of them. "Just because the dancers prayed to Dionysos and the monster was later killed, they say he did it."

Rumor convinced the village. The old grandmothers who neglected to say that the monster had been speared said instead it died from overeating. They gloried in the terrified expressions of the children.

"Let that be a lesson to you," they crowed, "to enjoy your tomotoes and cheese."

"Someday there won't be any rumors," whispered Silenos. He was trying to console Dionysos, who was sitting by a stream looking very forlorn after the triumph of the night before. "Everyone will have heard of your love for your followers, whether they're sprites or mortals, and your power to protect them."

Pan nodded his agreement and quickly produced some ripe figs he had chosen to sample from the baskets at Tanagra.

"Where do we go next?" asked Pan, resting on a lion.

"To Thebes," Dionysos replied, "because it is my home."

"Your home?" exclaimed Pan, leaping down. "I never knew you had one, except for Nysa and then Egypt, Arabia, India and Phrygia. Your home!"

"Yes, Pan," said Dionysos. "It was only because of Hera's wrath that I was forced to grow up in Nysa and wander through the east. My birthplace was Thebes. My mother was a Theban princess. Since she died, her name has been dishonored—by her own sisters. They spread the rumor that she lied when she said Zeus was her suitor. Now I am returning to confront the women who started this rumor and punish the king who does not recognize me as a god."

"Will you settle there afterwards?" gasped Pan.

"Oh, no," laughed Dionysos. "I haven't seen all of Greece yet."

Pan heaved a sigh of relief.

As soon as Dionysos arrived in Thebes, vines burst into bloom around Semele's tomb. At night a strange light glimmered. All over the countryside flowers and ivy sprouted. In honor of him there were maenads singing on the hills.

Return to Greece

In the marketplace of Thebes, two aged men were discussing the new occurrences. One was Cadmus, the father of Semele, who had long since given up his throne. The other was Teiresias, a blind prophet.

"Old man," Cadmus said to Teiresias, "I see that you have twined ivy around your head and have put on a fawnskin. I, too. Dionysos was my daughter's son and I will join him."

"Yes," said Teiresias. "Let's go together, in case one of us falls. While a chariot would be more convenient, for Dionysos we will happily forget our age."

"What is this?" cried Pentheus from the window of his palace. He was the son of one of Semele's sisters and now the king of Thebes. "You two holding those thyrsi are a ridiculous sight. There is no such person as Dionysos—god or mortal. He is buried with his mother."

"You are a fool," called Teiresias. "The god whom you mock will soon be the greatest god in Greece."

Pentheus swung about and disappeared into his large palace. Here a guard awaited him with a prisoner.

"I caught the man you wished," the guard began with embarrassment, "but he was so polite that I asked permission before I bound him. He smiled and told me kindly to take him to my king. One other thing, my lord—the women whom we threw into prison escaped. Their chains fell away, the bolts flew back, the doors opened and they're now dancing and frolicking in the mountains."

"How dare they?" cried Pentheus and strode up to the prisoner. "Where do you come from?"

"From the east."

"Why have you come to Thebes?"

The Spirit of Spring

"To teach the rites and dances of Dionysos."

"Dionysos? Who is he?"

"The son of Zeus."

"Oh," said Pentheus mockingly. "So there is an eastern Zeus who is sending new gods into Greece."

"No, he is the son of Zeus and the Theban princess, Semele."

"Take him to the stables," cried Pentheus in anger. "Let him dance in there."

"Beware," said the stranger. "The Dionysos whom you seek to thwart is not dead, and he will take revenge for this insult."

"Even if he were alive, do you think the son of my mother's sister could have more power than I . . . I, the king of Thebes?"

No sooner had the guard led the man away than a terrible earthquake shattered the palace. Marble columns crashed onto the floor like trees that had been hit with an axe. Rafters fell on top of them. Stones reeled and shot about like meteors. Pentheus rushed to hold onto the prisoner. He struggled with what he thought was the insolent follower of Dionysos, but he fought against a bull, which butted and kicked and roared. The flame on Semele's tomb near the palace grew brighter, and Pentheus cried out for water. Soon the whole palace seemed on fire. Then he spied the man again. He ran to the courtyard. He took up his sword and slashed out in all directions. It was only when the earthquake had ceased that he saw he had demolished the stable. The man was standing unharmed behind him.

Before Pentheus could say a word, messengers came

in with the news that the sisters of Semele had joined Dionysos' band and now they, too, were dancing furiously in the mountains.

"Would you care to see them dancing?" said the prisoner.

"Would I?" cried Pentheus wildly. "And catch them at their evil pursuits."

"You will see," said the man.

Twilight had brought a golden glow to the forest as the man led Pentheus, disguised as a Theban woman, up the slopes of the mountains. They halted in a small hollow. Nearby, groups of maenads were busy feeding woodland animals, sewing on foxskins and weaving flowers into garlands, but although Pentheus peered everywhere, he was so intent on beholding wickedness that he could not see a single maenad.

"Is there no way I can glimpse these terrible women?" he finally whispered.

The man from the east then caught a tall pine by its branches and dragged it down to the ground. In the pale light of the woodland, his features shone clearly. It was Dionysos. He beckoned to the Theban king. Pentheus eagerly crawled onto the sturdy boughs. Gradually, Dionysos released his hold. Little by little the tree slid through his hands, and then, once above the other trees, flung itself up to its full height. Pentheus clutched the topmost branch, in full view of the whole mountain.

Then Dionysos cried, "Maenads! This is the king who mocks us, who would break our thyrsi and tear up our dancing places. Vengeance must be had—otherwise we will be forced from Greece by kings such as

The Spirit of Spring

this and made to wander over the earth, a homeless
god and a homeless band. Now we must show our
power."

There was a flash of fire. Its awful flame illuminated
the maenads coming down the mountain, inspired by
their god. They were prepared now as never before and
they came like an army. With boulders, with stones,
they tried to dislodge the evil king from his perch.
When these failed, with their bare hands they tore
down the tree and killed him, and his own mother
unknowingly dealt the final blow.

"Woe to both of you, mother and son," Dionysos
cried in a terrible voice. "You, mother, because you
did not believe that your sister, Semele, gave birth to
a god. And you, Pentheus, because you did not accept
him, although you had the chance. Let your fate be a
lesson. Come, maenads, we have gained our place in
Greece. No god or mortal can ever drive us away."

The sprites mounted their lynxes and leopards, and
touching their flanks with sprays of bright green leaves,
they trotted off through the shadowy forest.

CHAPTER SIX

The Spirit of Spring

*Dionysos dropped to his knees on the beach
beside the young girl, marveling at her beauty.*

ONE DAY, LONG AFTER THE EVENTS AT THEBES, DIONYSOS was walking along the seashore in a cheerful mood. He had swayed the mainland as he had swayed the lands in the east. Now, despite the wrath of Hera and jealous mortal kings, he and his woodland troop were accepted everywhere, or as Pan said, with a more practical eye, "Everywhere the vine grew."

He strolled along blithely, small flowers opening up all around him. Suddenly he caught sight of a black ship speeding toward the coast. The men on board were clutching their landing ladders, and Dionysos looked more closely. Their vessel reminded him of the little moon-boat that had carried him and his satyrs and maenads so gallantly to Egypt. In a rush, the high expectations of the forest sprites came back to him, the delighted faces of those who had joined his crew on the briefest notice, who had deserted their meadows and forests, and who had without hesitation sailed off over a watery path to strange and exotic lands.

"All we have done recently has been to travel

The Spirit of Spring

around the mainland of Greece," he murmured to himself. "I wonder. . . ."

He was immersed in a new thought. Meanwhile, the ship had stolen up to the shore, and everyone on board was gazing upon him with fascination. Never had they seen such a man. His black hair tumbled over his broad shoulders, and his body had a strength that was almost immortal—like that of Zeus. What a price he would bring in the slave markets!

In a moment they had leapt upon him. They were the infamous Tyrrhenian pirates, hated and feared by peoples of every land. With a swift wind, Hera had sent their ship careening across the sea to this stretch of coast, confident that they would detect Dionysos rambling along the bluffs, carrying his golden winecup, and spirit him off far away from Greece.

Dionysos let them drag him on board, but he only smiled at their feeble attempts to bind his hands and feet.

"I would like to go to Naxos," the god said suddenly, as though the thought had just occurred to him.

"Naxos!" The pirates shook their heads malevolently while they struggled with the bonds, which kept dropping on the deck in a useless heap.

"You will not see Greece anymore. You are going to the slave markets," they cried. "To the east!"

"Not again," said Dionysos lightly. "I've already been."

There was an unsettling stillness after he said this. The pirates looked around, and then in terror jumped for their oars. But it was to no avail, for the blunt-edged oars had turned into delicate thyrsi, which circled in their hands merrily.

The Spirit of Spring

Then the changes that had taken place in the most unlikely parts of earth, on wind-swept coasts and barren deserts, began to take place all over the dark-prowed ship. Ivy twirled up the mast and a grapevine joined it, and together the two green creepers stretched out over the sail and burst into flower. Clusters of grapes soon were swinging across the top in the breeze. Buds sprang out of the black boards and were quickly followed by woodland flowers, and everywhere there was the pungent smell of spring.

"Where is he?" yelled the pirates.

In the confusion they had lost sight of Dionysos, and when they spotted him again it was but indistinctly through the leafy sprays. He was reclining in the prow like an oriental king, wreathed from head to toe in his favorite flowers and waving a thyrsus in the direction of Naxos.

"Put to shore! Put to shore!" the pirates cried.

They were rushing back and forth, pulling at the vines and throwing the grape clusters over the side. While any village in Greece would have been delighted by such a harvest, where one grape cluster dropped and another sprouted immediately in its place, fully grown and ripe, the pirates were frantic.

"To shore! To shore!"

It was too late. Dionysos had turned himself into a lion and was crouched by the stern, roaring ferociously. He was calling to his shaggy bears, his spotted lynxes, his glossy panthers and his terrible tigers to join him. The whole pack landed on the deck from the air with a loud thud and began chasing the pirates all over the ship, in and among the flowers, setting up a fearful din and slipping on the grapes.

The Spirit of Spring

loud shout.

"Enoi!"

This time the satyrs, maenads and sileni tripped aboard.

"Where will we find him next?" puffed Silenos to Pan—he had been puzzled earlier by Dionysos' sudden disappearance.

Having found their leader, everyone began to revel at once. The sileni backed up against the familiar flowers and plants and played their instruments madly, which boomed and shrilled and clacked.

"Who wreathed the tholepins of the oars?" cried Bright-Eyes above the music.

"I did," said Thyrbas, although he had not done so at all. Then he threw a wreath around a confused pirate's neck. Bright-Eyes followed with another.

The festivities were too much for the pirates. The ship rocked dangerously. They were dancing. To the sound of flutes and drums and tympanums, they started to whirl more and more gaily, and then, unable to find space enough to complete their steps, they spread out into the sea. The forest creatures ran to the side to see what had happened. The sea was still filled with dancers and tumblers, but they were not pirates, for Dionysos had turned them all into dolphins.

Dionysos watched with pleasure his new breed of creatures, which burst into the air, did a dance turn and disappeared again, then came up for applause, spouting water in a beautiful arc, which the sun turned into a rainbow. They received overjoyed applause.

"Dionysos," the woodland spirits cried, "where are we going—it's spring?"

The Spirit of Spring

"On a holiday," he replied, "through the Greek islands."

They sailed away, dolphins tumbling and splashing beneath them and vines ripening and blossoming above.

When Dionysos and his band reached Naxos, the first of the evening stars was pushing through the purplish sky, shedding its pale light over the beaches and hills before them as if it were marking the island. On the ship the maenads tapped their feet in anticipation and occasionally clapped a tambourine. Something thrilling was about to happen. The woodland spirits felt it.

With great fanfare the ship was moored. However happy Dionysos' followers were to be at sea, they were always happier to be on land. They lined up behind their leader, clutching their ivy, their vines, their thyrsi, their winecups, their musical instruments and their wreaths. As soon as Dionysos' foot touched the shores of Naxos, they flew after him.

The god led them off, not down flower-strewn paths to inland groves but away over the cliffs. Even on the jagged rock the maenads frisked and frolicked. The satyrs capered. Panthers, leopards and lynxes raced beside them and pushed against one another for the privilege of rubbing Dionysos' legs with their shanks, behaving like dogs on an outing with their master.

"How many new creatures do we have now, Dionysos?" cried Pan. He had been enchanted with the dolphins, had watched them endlessly, and now he was counting clumsily on his fingers. "Let's see— panthers from India, bats from Orchomenus, dolphins from. . . ."

The Spirit of Spring

With a whoop the satyrs approached an unexpected white beach, with a shout the maenads joined them, with a roar the animals flew through the air to be the first on its soft surface, and with a whisper Dionysos halted them all, "Someone is already here."

Just above the wave line, a girl lay sleeping. Wrapped in a silk robe as blue as the sea at midday, she was slumbering soundly on the beach that was to have held their dancing. A pillow of red roses lay under her head and looked like a silken cushion on which her radiant hair was being displayed to the moon watching from above. Her tresses had fallen free from a knot of ribbons, and the stars had charged them with fabulous light as though they wished the soft golden strands to illuminate the pale and wondrous face to the waiting night.

Dionysos had dropped to his knees on the beach beside the young girl, marveling at her beauty. He gently drew her up by her shoulders and the girl awoke quietly in his arms.

"Theseus," she whispered in a strangely musical voice. "Theseus?"

She was obviously an island girl, whose ears had long heard the poetry of winds, waves, birds and breezes, and whose speech has naturally assumed the same lilting expression. And she was obviously a princess, a mortal one, for she was arrayed in the most finely woven robes and the most precious jewels that could be found on earth.

"Where did she come from?" whispered Pan. "There is no kingdom here."

He would have gone further had not Silenos nudged him. Soundlessly, covering their tambourines with

The Spirit of Spring

their fawnskins, the satyrs, maenads and sileni withdrew.

"Theseus has left," said Dionysos.

"Theseus has left!" the girl echoed softly. She suddenly realized she was in Dionysos' arms and pulled away in dismay. "Theseus has left me on Naxos?"

"I told him to," said Dionysos hurriedly, lest the fragile princess dissolve into tears. "I came here while you were asleep—with the goddess Athena—and we pursuaded him to go back to his city. Although he was strong and brave, he was a mortal . . . and you. . . ."

Here Dionysos dropped his voice and spoke fervently, "And you are so beautiful, Ariadne. I know your name . . . I know what has happened, how you betrayed your father by giving Theseus a ball of thread to bring him back safely through the winding corridors of the labyrinth. I even know what you dreamed alone in the gardens on Crete, how you loved the swallows that flew over the island on their way to Egypt, and how you longed to follow. And I know when the Athenian prince, Theseus, came to your enclosed world, how you longed to go off with him to see the purplish mountains around Athens, and the horses grazing on the plains. You did, didn't you?"

The princess nodded in wonder.

"You will see them," said Dionysos, "and you will not even remember that you were once to be queen over them, for with me you will rule over a much grander kingdom."

From his long robes the god drew out a crown he had brought from India and put it on her shining head. He took her hand and felt as though he had

The Spirit of Spring

touched the whole mortal world, made up of endless **111** dreams and longings, which to him seemed as beautiful as the flowers that bloomed there—although to any other god they would have seemed only as perishable. The girl trembled.

"Who are you?" she asked.

"Dionysos."

With his other hand the god beckoned to the maenads. Moving gracefully and singing a light melody, they emerged one by one from behind the cliffs and rocks where they had been hiding. Their fawnskins were neat, and their wreaths were unexpectedly trim. Soon the satyrs joined them, trailing vine sprays, flowers and ivy. In small groups at the edge of the beach, the sileni appeared. They tested their tambourines and tapped their cymbals, listening carefully to make sure they were in tune.

"What a magical people," breathed Ariadne. "Just a moment ago the beach was as deserted as my chamber in the palace, and now. . . ."

Now it seemed as if every being of the forest were there on the strand checking an instrument or clearing a throat, preparing for the overture to an evening of dance. Then there was the clash of cymbals and the chattering of castanets. The maenads leapt into the air and twirled and twisted, soared and spun. Around them, the satyrs broke into intricate circles.

Ariadne was enthralled. Never, not even on her own exquisite dancing floor on Crete, had she seen such dancing, which seemed to take place up in the moonlight rather than on the beach, as though the sprites had wings. Never had the princess heard such

The Spirit of Spring

enchanting music, which swept through her like the scent of violets and roses, drawing her into the delirium of unrestrained movement as the scent of flowers on Crete had drawn her into the delirium of early spring. She forgot everything. When Dionysos stood before her and invited her to dance, she could hardly wait to feel the world under her feet and the god guiding her steps.

"Dionysos!" she whispered excitedly. "Do you dance?"

As she spoke, there were peals of airy laughter, which were not harsh but soft—like moonbeams—giving a warm luster to the forest sprites' feelings.

"*Do* you dance, Dionysos?" they echoed.

Dionysos whirled Ariadne to her feet and they started away, down the beach, with Pan, Silenos, Bright-Eyes, Joyous Disturbance and all the animals in jubilant pursuit. The god and the princess danced together until the night fled, and then they danced some more—in the groves, on the beaches, atop the mountains, down in the valleys—until the whole of the island had felt the ecstasy of their spinning steps. The woodland band who followed joyously behind were surprised and later astonished, for no other maiden had ever before danced at the side of Dionysos.

They were married that day by Silenos. Pan played his pipes, and although the sprites stood still for the wedding, the island almost sank with their celebrations later on, which continued until Dionysos disappeared with his bride in a magnificent chariot from the top of the highest mountain. And soon after, all Greece was their dancing floor.

The Spirit of Spring

Ascent to Olympus

CHAPTER SEVEN

"Hephestos," said Dionysos. "You have finished your revels and your wine. We are home now."

*I*T WAS ALWAYS BEAUTIFUL WEATHER ON THE MOUNTAIN of the gods, and the high winds, snow and sleet never appeared in their recognizable, physical forms as they did on earth to plague mortals. Nevertheless, Mount Olympus seemed to go through its own seasonal disturbances—as it was doing at present in Zeus's throne room. While the sky was clear outside, so clear that the king of the gods could easily distinguish the nostrils and manes of the sun's steeds, a wintry atmosphere prevailed there.

The queen of the gods was sitting on an elaborate throne, which was draped with purple coverlets and cushions. She was moving these backwards and forwards angrily, for they no longer seemed comfortable, as she had been sitting on them for weeks. Zeus sat on his majestic throne beside her, staring into the magnificence of his counsel hall and out the window.

They had spent the past weeks conversing about earth—all of earth—and it had been a very trying experience for them both. Neither had mentioned Dionysos. Earth was so different now, since his arrival, that it

The Spirit of Spring

was almost impossible to discuss it with any pleasure, or even at all, without noting the newcomer.

Finally Hera remarked casually, "And how is he . . . the delight of mortals?"

"Who?"

"Dionysos."

"Oh," said Zeus. "Dionysos. . . . Recently he turned the Tyrrhenian pirates into dolphins."

The queen of the gods replied frostily, "He uses his powers in a frivolous fashion."

Then she added with dignity, "And so do his followers. Just the other day a maenad rapped a statue of me with her thyrsus. . . ."

The king of the gods covered a smile with his scepter.

"Zeus," said Hera warningly, "he is an upstart and he is making a mockery of my entire realm. The women who used to worship me are now off in the hills, racing around bowls of wine—this miraculous new drink that they say has more power than nectar. Since he came. . . ."

"Hera . . ." said Zeus testily.

"Since he came, the children have had no mothers. . . ." said Hera.

"Hera!"

"They're away playing with fawns and fox cubs. . . ." she shrilled.

"Hera!" Zeus broke in. "Who are you to talk about children and mothers? You threw your own son Hephestos off the ramparts of Mount Olympus! Thetis, the sea nymph, took him into her cave to nurse him after his fall. . . ."

Ascent to Olympus

"She takes in all stray children," snapped Hera.

"Then she sent him back to Mount Olympus," Zeus raised his voice in exasperation, "and told him to forgive you."

"He should have," agreed Hera. "He was so hideous and deformed, I don't see why he expected me to . . ."

"But you were his mother and you are sitting on that throne now, and probably will forever, because he didn't forgive you. He gave you an enchanted present out of spite, so that when you sank delightedly into it, you couldn't get up!"

"Zeus!" cried Hera in tears.

"And I do not see how you can say Dionysos is turning mortals into bad mothers. You. . . ."

"Oh, Zeus," wailed Hera. "I don't care about Dionysos! Can't anyone find Hephestos?"

The conversation ended abruptly with the arrival of Hermes, who had been staying in Arcadia with his mother ever since Hera sat down on the throne.

"Zeus! You won't believe what's taking place!"

There was the clash of cymbals in the distance, the blare of horns and the ringing of timbrels, and into the throne room sped the other gods and goddesses —Apollo, Poseidon, Athena, Artemis, Aphrodite. They were all murmuring.

"Zeus! An extraordinary procession from earth is arriving! Usually they just go to our temples. We don't think anyone has ever before attempted to. . . ."

"Oh, no!" shrieked Hera.

"Do you think they will get lost?" asked Hermes apprehensively. "Perhaps I had better. . . ."

The Spirit of Spring

"Oh, they'll find their way," Hera reassured him.

She had not watched their zigzagging movements over the countryside without noticing that they always found their way as surely as ivy always found its way into the light.

"Maybe he'll bring his wife," said Hermes hopefully.

"He can't," said Hera. "She was killed."

"Ariadne?"

"Yes, in a fight with some mortal king. Didn't you see that new group of stars in the heavens? They're the Corona Arborealis. It's her crown. He put it there when she died—he does the most *imaginative* things." Hera smiled endearingly at the gods.

There was the clatter of hooves on the gold-paved road, and the drumming of bare feet, as the band came nearer.

"On earth, everyone is re-enacting at festivals the things he does. Drama, it's called. D–R–A–M–A. While he does whatever he wants wherever he pleases, mortals limit their renditions to circular areas—threshing floors and the sides of hills."

"And I suppose," she said to Zeus bitingly, "I will have to receive him, since he appears now to be coming here."

"If he comes to the throne room," said Zeus, "I don't see how. . . ."

"All visitors come to the throne room," said Hermes without thinking.

"But maybe he will drive us out of the throne room!" Hera said, and glared at Zeus and his messenger. "With his thyrsus!"

Hera was helpless with rage. She had hoped, rather

Ascent to Olympus

dreamed, of meeting Dionysos someday at the summit of her power. With a display of magic she would have caused him and his vines and his followers to disappear forever, and the world would have gone slowly back to the way it was before, when there had been no grapes, no harvests, no laughter, and everybody had envied the gods their nectar instead of marveling over their own cup of wine.

"Can't any one of you find Hephestos?" she railed at the gods and goddesses.

"Ares went to earth for him," said Hermes soothingly, "but they had a skirmish. Ares forgot that while he was the god of war, Hephestos was the god of artillery, and when he tried to bring back your son by force, he was almost destroyed. I am sorry, Hera, truly . . . but nobody has been able to persuade Hephestos to come back to Mount Olympus."

Hera looked crestfallen. For weeks she had remained on the enchanted throne, and that was much too long for anyone to contemplate a career such as hers. As the shrieks of jollity outside came closer and closer, the faces of the nymphs she had turned into beasts, the faces of the men she had driven mad, coursed through her mind. Furthermore, she began to notice that of all the faces around her, not one was as concerned as it should have been.

She started to point this out only to be interrupted by a boisterous noise like the brooks all over Greece gurgling up and cascading over their banks in early spring—or a noise like an unsuppressed peal of laughter. The gods and goddesses hurried to the windows. Hera tried to join them, but fell back with a jolt, for the throne would not let her go.

The Spirit of Spring

The forest creatures, with their hair streaming free, their hooves sparkling, their robes swirling and their wreaths dropping flowers and petals in a fragrant cloud behind them, ran up the steps of the palace and headed unswervingly for Zeus's throne room. Before anyone knew what was happening, the maenads, satyrs and sileni had jumped over the bronze threshold and were prancing about inside, pointing at the ceiling and peering at the floors, chattering to everyone blithely.

"Why, this looks like the palace in India!" cried Revel.

"It's much more beautiful . . ." replied Summer Bloom.

"King Midas had one of these!"

A satyr pulled an embroidered cushion from Hera's throne, but then, because she looked unhappy, he gave her a fawnskin and tucked it behind her back.

"These thrones," said Joyous Disturbance, "are so uncomfortable. When you come to earth. . . ."

Then he handed her a tambourine and ran off to find Bright-Eyes, who was wrapping Apollo in flowers and vines.

"Do you dance?"

Gathering themselves, the gods and goddesses tore after the sprites, trying to herd them out, questioning their right to be on Mount Olympus in the first place, much less in the palace of the king of the gods, informing them that all cymbals must be left at the gates —and all animals. Crash! *Grrrr.* Yes, absolutely all cymbals and. . . .

Zeus, discovering it was impossible to stand still, located his messenger and cried above the din, "Do you feel a desire to dance?"

Ascent to Olympus

Hermes nodded, without even attempting to shout. The turmoil had reached unparalleled heights. A host of flirtatious maenads, distraught gods, friendly sileni, capricious satyrs and wrathful goddesses were dashing for differing reasons around the throne of Hera. The dance—of sorts—was gathering momentum, the music was quickening, the queen of the gods was deathly pale, when suddenly into the maelstrom someone cried out, "Quiet!"

Everyone stopped, poised on their tiptoes, and the silence was as overpowering as the earlier pandemonium. The gods and goddesses did not know who had spoken. They looked up and saw a black-haired god —he must be a god—with a winecup. The stranger strode into the throne room, quickly, leading a donkey by its halter, and there on its back was Hephestos, fast asleep and dreaming.

Before the speechless deities, Dionysos awoke the god.

"Hephestos! You have finished your revels and your wine. We are home now. . . . Hephestos?"

The lame god blinked groggily and happily, as if he were not sure where home was, and slid off the donkey. He looked around and saw Hera and limped up as fast as he was able.

"Mother!" he cried. "I have had the most exciting time and I have been with the most brilliant people. . . ."

With no recollection of the charmed throne, he held out his arms and Hera came easily into them.

"Mother!" he said breathlessly. "This is Dionysos. I met him on earth. We had some refreshment and. . . ."

"You look familiar," said Hera unsteadily.

The Spirit of Spring

"I'm sure," said Dionysos, smiling, still holding the donkey. He bowed to her. "How do you do. . . ."

Then Hera smiled, too, and suddenly put her arms around their shoulders.

"Welcome, Dionysos!" she said. "What can I give you for bringing my son home to Olympus when all others failed? Is there anything you wish?"

"To come home, also," replied Dionysos, looking around him. "Once I thought that Thebes would be my home, but now I know that Olympus . . . that Olympus. . . ."

". . . has always been your home," finished Hera. "Your wish is granted. And now, let us celebrate!" The queen of the gods stepped lightly onto the footstool of the empty throne. "All of us!"

There was a shout of approval. Zeus made his way through his enthusiastic visitors to greet his son.

"How did you ever manage to bring Hephestos back to Mount Olympus?" he exclaimed to Dionysos. "Of all the things you have ever done, this is the most stupendous."

"We were having a woodland party," began Dionysos, "and Hephestos joined it. He danced and sang. Then he danced some more. He didn't ever want to stop. You know he is lame, and so when he did stop, he went immediately to sleep. I asked him where he wished to go, as we couldn't leave him there in the forest, and he happily said, 'Home!' I asked him where that was and he replied, 'Mount Olympus!' Thereupon we all decided to take him."

Zeus laughed uproariously.

"You see, Hermes," he cried to his messenger.

Ascent to Olympus

"Now there's nowhere he hasn't been. . . ." Zeus shook out a creeper some maenad had tossed around his neck. ". . . With the grapevine."

"He hasn't been to Hades," objected Hermes.

"Oh, he'll go," laughed Zeus over his shoulder.

The king of the gods led his family off to the banqueting hall, where the maenads, satyrs and sileni were seated at the long table among the gods and goddesses—the panthers, leopards and lynxes crouched underneath.

Then the whole assemblage—the powers of heaven and earth—wildly feted Dionysos. The woodland god and his sprites drank new wine. Although the gods and goddesses drank only nectar, they drank it out of wine-cups.

Late, late that evening, Zeus and Hera remained a moment together in the throne room. The sprites were back in their forests on earth, tucked away in their grassy hollows and flowering glens and dingles, dreaming of their revels on Mount Olympus. Hephestos was back in his own palace. And Dionysos was asleep in the guest chambers of their palace.

"I think this is a one-day vine," said Hera, thoughtfully, looking at the long creeper that was still around Zeus's neck.

"A what?"

"A one-day vine. They flower for one day, no matter what the season, whenever Dionysos has been present. Zeus. . . . Where was Nysa?"

Although Hera had considered asking Zeus this question many times in the past, she had not done so, knowing that it would have to wait. She had not known then, however, that it would have to wait a long time, for her query was part of a bulk of questions that can never fully be answered. Where was anyone's childhood spent, in what remote land—and Dionysos' above all? Where had he first carried the thyrsus and the winecup? Where had he first learned to cultivate the vine? Where had the satyrs, maenads and sileni originally come from, who sailed off to Egypt and then marched triumphantly through Asia and on up to Olympus behind a leader they knew was a god? Even Zeus himself could not tell her.

"Nysa?" the king of the gods said vaguely. "I don't know."

Zeus had forgotten—he had sent Dionysos there so long ago—and the exact location of Nysa was lost forever, although when men discover where the first wild grapevine was cultivated and where the first red grapejuice flowed into an amphora, they will know that Dionysos' nursery could not have been far from that place.

Zeus and Hera walked through the deserted throne room, picking their way among the flowers, ivy and vines scattered over the mosaics, their blooms still brighter than the precious stones.

"Is it true that panthers and sphinxes are metamorphosed maenads?" asked Hera.

"A rumor," replied Zeus. He paused by the window.

"There will be a new route soon," he said, looking out, "more colorful than the gold route, the amber route or even the ivory route. . . ."

". . . when wine in slender amphoras begins to travel around the world."

Zeus nodded.

Ascent to Olympus

"He was born to be a joy to mortals," he said happily.

"That he has been," said Hera with a smile, and they, too, went off to sleep.

Dionysos stayed with Zeus and Hera for a spell in their palace while his own was being built by Hephestos, who could work on things other than artillery with his flaming tools. As soon as the magnificent mansion was finished, Dionysos walked through its halls and stared out its tall windows at earth.

"Oh, Ariadne," he sighed sadly, unable to continue gazing upon the dancing groves they had enjoyed together.

The god looked instead over the fertile lands to which he had been with his vines and flowers. The only place he couldn't find was Nysa. Suddenly, he remembered the Hyades.

"Where could they be now?" exclaimed Dionysos.

That evening he had a meeting with Zeus, and before the moon had risen to its highest peak, the night was a shade brighter than it had ever been before. All the gods and goddesses rushed outside to see what had happened, only to be told by Hermes that Dionysos had just put his five nurses in the stars over his palace, so that they could be near him always.

No sooner had the Hyades faded away with the dawn than Dionysos leapt up and hurried back to earth. He greeted the maenads and satyrs gaily, he laughed at the prancing goats, he sampled the peasants' wine. But he sped past—past the places of beautiful dancing, past the vineyards—until he came to the

The Spirit of Spring

golden groves of Troezen. There among the orange and lemon trees was the entrance to the underworld. It was a sinister cave in the middle of a beautiful grotto, overhung with cool leafy boughs and flowers.

He smiled at the satyrs and maenads who had naturally followed him, and then disappeared down the gaping entrance with his ivy, his grapevines, his myrtle and his winecup.

"Where on earth is he going?" cried Silenos, peering after him.

"He's not going anywhere on earth. He's going—or has just gone—to the land of the dead," quavered Pan. "I'm glad he didn't ask us."

"Is there no place he won't go?" exclaimed Silenos.

"It will probably burst into flower," retorted Pan loyally, and added, "Let's wait for him here."

"Yes, let's," agreed Silenos and stretched out and went to sleep, delighted with the warm breezes that stirred up the scent of flowers.

Meanwhile, Dionysos hurried through the dank passageways, which had never felt the warmth or gaiety of light. The only other movements beside his were the shades, the spirits of those who had died, rippling back and forth restlessly. They were trying to reach the opening to the grotto, to flutter there—not to cross its boundaries—and smell the fruits and flowers. However, as soon as they saw Dionysos, draped with vines and blossoms, they changed their courses and streamed back the other way, like fish in the midnight depths of the water.

Charon, the grizzled boatman of that region, asked Dionysos what he was doing when the god suddenly appeared on the banks of the river Styx, with a host of diaphanous followers.

"Can you ferry me across?" asked Dionysos. "I am going to see Hades."

The old boatman was so shaken to see myrtle, ivy, pine boughs and grapevines flourishing as if they had been in the land of the living instead of the land of the dead that he let Dionysos board. He gave a great heave, for Dionysos was no shade, and the boat, heavily laden, lurched across the black river.

"Mind you, watch that dog," said the boatman. The green around Dionysos' mantle stirred the boatman with dim longings of other rivers and other passengers, who had long ago on earth boarded his ship with laughter and garlands of flowers.

"Wait for me," said Dionysos as they pushed through the prickly reeds to the shore. "I will soon be back."

"I hope . . ." said Charon gloomily.

In a very short time Dionysos arrived at the huge palace where the king of the dead lived with his young queen, Persephone. There by the towering portal crouched their watchdog, Cerberus. All three of its massive heads were raised, quivering with anticipation. All three pairs of eyes stared into the murk. Likewise all its ears were cocked, and its scarlet tongues slipped back and forth, up and down its bloodthirsty jaws. Upon seeing Dionysos, the dog drew itself up to its full height, blinked and started to wag its tail.

"There! There!" said Dionysos playfully, scratching it behind its three sets of ears, one after another.

The dog rolled its heads all to one side, its tongues

lolled out in pleasure, and Dionysos gave it one last pat and passed by, leaving the beast and the shades wistfully looking after him. He soon found himself in a splendid throne room, as big as Zeus's on Mount Olympus, facing the king who ruled over one-third of the world—the third beneath the earth.

"I have come," said Dionysos without ado, to both Hades and his queen, "for two mortal princesses who died—Semele and Ariadne."

There was a long, rippling silence. Other gods had loved mortals and others had even had mortal mothers, but very few had ventured to Hades' realm to claim them, once they had finished their allotted time on earth.

"I am the god of woodlands," said Dionysos, "of vineyards, of harvests, of song, of wine, of laughter, of. . . ."

"Yes, yes," said Hades thoughtfully. Rumors of this new god had traveled even to the land of the dead, and the rumors had dealt mostly with his vast wealth. Unlike the other gods, he was worshiped all over the world—in Egypt, in India, in Asia and in Greece; in fact, everywhere the vine grew—and everyone in these places brought him gifts.

Hades regarded Dionysos cunningly. "You are a god, and you are lord over all the things you mentioned. I will give you back your wife and mother, although the situation is irregular, but you must give me in return whatever I ask of you."

"Certainly," said Dionysos.

"You promise," pressed the king harshly.

"I do . . ." replied Dionysos.

Ascent to Olympus

"Then give me the one thing you love best on earth."

"I will offer you a choice," said Dionysos, "since out of all the things I have been given, I have loved three the most—the myrtle, the ivy, and the pine."

"What?" roared Hades.

He had never even considered the wealth of earth —the wealth that never gives out and can be loved without stint, the treasury of wild flowers, plants and animals that fills up anew every season and seems to overflow with the return of spring.

"Which plant do you wish?" asked Dionysos.

The king of the dead looked grimmer than ever.

"It doesn't really matter, does it?" he said. "They're all the same, aren't they?"

"I have kept my part of the bargain," said Dionysos warningly.

Hades thought for a moment about which he would choose. Then he cried, "All right! I'll take the myrtle! You take your wife and mother, and leave instantly! Do not let your presence in my kingdom continue to remind me what a fool I have been . . . asking the god of woodlands and vineyards for his most prized possession. Go!"

With that he summoned Ariadne and Semele.

"Watch out for the dog!" cried his lovely queen, Persephone, with one last, longing look at Dionysos.

Semele and Ariadne came forward, and Dionysos led them away down the dark corridors, past Cerberus who fawned at his feet and howled when he left. They crossed the river with the baffled boatman. They gathered speed as they neared the entrance, and then, with a final spring, all three left the shades and the

The Spirit of Spring

land of darkness forever and burst into the daylight.

"How wonderful!" cried Ariadne, gazing at the color of earth.

"How beautiful!" said Semele, but she was looking with amazement at the extraordinary creatures surrounding them.

The maenads, satyrs and sileni were playing trumpets. They had hoped the earsplitting racket would help Dionysos find his way back, however far down he had gone. Now that he was again in their midst, they threw down their instruments—fiery-faced and spent.

"Dionysos . . ." they puffed. "Ariadne . . . Semele. . . ."

"We're in Troezen at last," cried Dionysos, as their eyes swept over the radiant countryside.

"Troezen!" exclaimed Ariadne.

She seemed to remember Troezen from long ago—the name was filled with bright images of orange groves, little blue islands and endless bays.

"Dionysos . . ." she cried, but when he looked up she forgot her query.

Dionysos had pulled aside the boughs of the grotto. There a chariot was waiting, drawn by a lion and a stag, to bear them away to Mount Olympus.

"Pan! Silenos!" Dionysos called.

Pan and Silenos had crept behind a tree and through the foliage were watching their pupil's return from Hades.

"Pan! Silenos!"

"He doesn't have his myrtle anymore . . ." whispered Silenos.

"He must have traded it for them. . . ." said Pan.

Ascent to Olympus

"Yes. . . ."

The sprites could not bear to say good-bye, and as Dionysos helped his family into his chariot, and the trumpets started playing, they stumbled away through the underbrush. Not even looking at each other, they picked up their separate paths to their own forests.

That was the way with all the woodland creatures. The love of their own land was the strongest pull on their frail beings. While they had loved Dionysos and had served him faithfully, once the glorious deeds were done and the golden songs were sung, the sweet lure of their homelands stretched over the miles to prickle the backs of their necks and rub the windows of their minds clear to sparkle with a forgotten view. All the horned beings, the tailed ones and the barefooted ones departed from Troezen and set out for the deep forests, the flowering ravines and the sunlit meadows from which they had first come.

Pan returned to his beloved pasturelands in Arcadia, to play his pipes, frighten the shepherds and scatter their flocks of sheep.

Silenos soon could be heard all over Greece. He climbed back onto his mountain and lounged on its crest as though it were a throne from which he could bombard his subjects below with vituperation and bloodcurdling admonition.

He rent apart the green fabric of the mountain slopes with his sermons on virtue, but it was sewn back together again quickly. The birds still yanked and pulled the twigs and vines for their airy houses, and the red fox continued to nurse her young. Silenos

The Spirit of Spring

had become too windy for the wind itself to tolerate as it flashed by.

"Why are you so concerned with preaching the right and wrong," it roared, "when you could be aiding the peasants in their unending routine of surviving the winter and harvesting the spring?"

Silenos bellowed with laughter, continued his tirade, and kept his seat astride the windswept peak.

"Dionysos will do that," he cried, "from Mount Olympus."

Ascent to Olympus

GLOSSARY

AMBROSIA	The food of the immortals
AMPHORA	A long, clay jar for storing or shipping wine
CHITON	A short, knee-length garment
CLAPPER	A musical instrument that makes a clapping noise
HIMATION	A long robe
ICHOR	The blood that flows in the immortals' veins
LYRE	A musical instrument resembling a harp
MOUNT OLYMPUS	The home of the gods
NECTAR	The drink of the immortals
NYSA	The enchanted gardens where Dionysos spent his childhood
STYX	The river that flows through the underworld
THYRSUS	A staff twined with vines and ivy, carried by the followers of Dionysos
TIMBREL	A hand drum resembling a tambourine
TYMPANUM	A drum